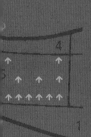

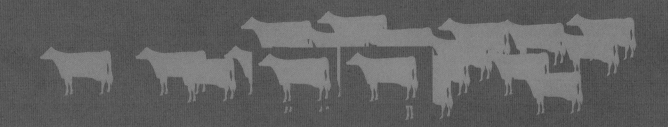

ART AND COOK
LOVE FOOD, LIVE DESIGN AND DREAM ART

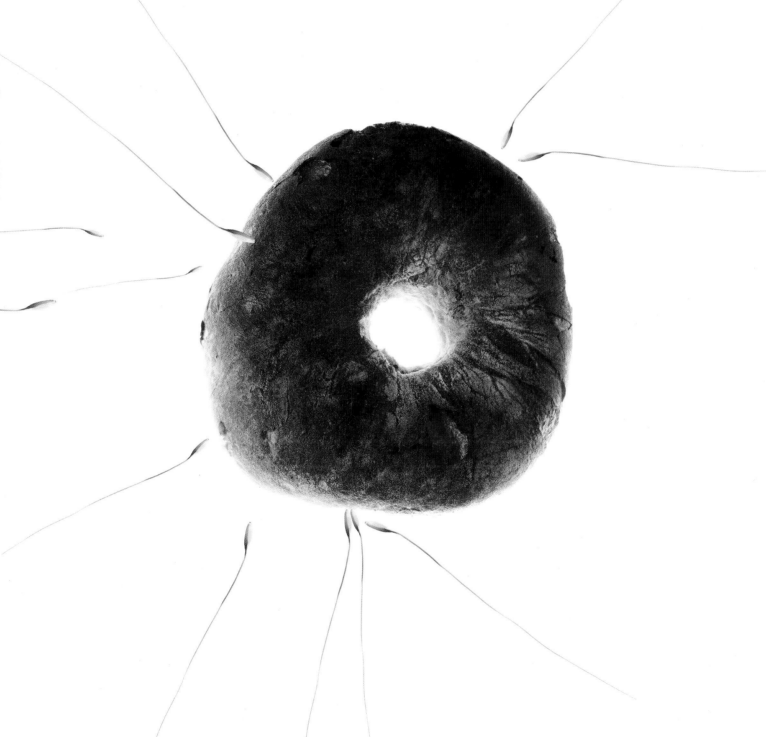

CEO & PHOTOGRAPHER: ALLAN BEN

ART DIRECTOR & DESIGNER: EMMANUEL PALETZ

RECIPE DEVELOPER: EINAV GEFEN DUBNIKOV

FOOD STYLISTS: LIRON MELLER, MELANIE R. UNDERWOOD

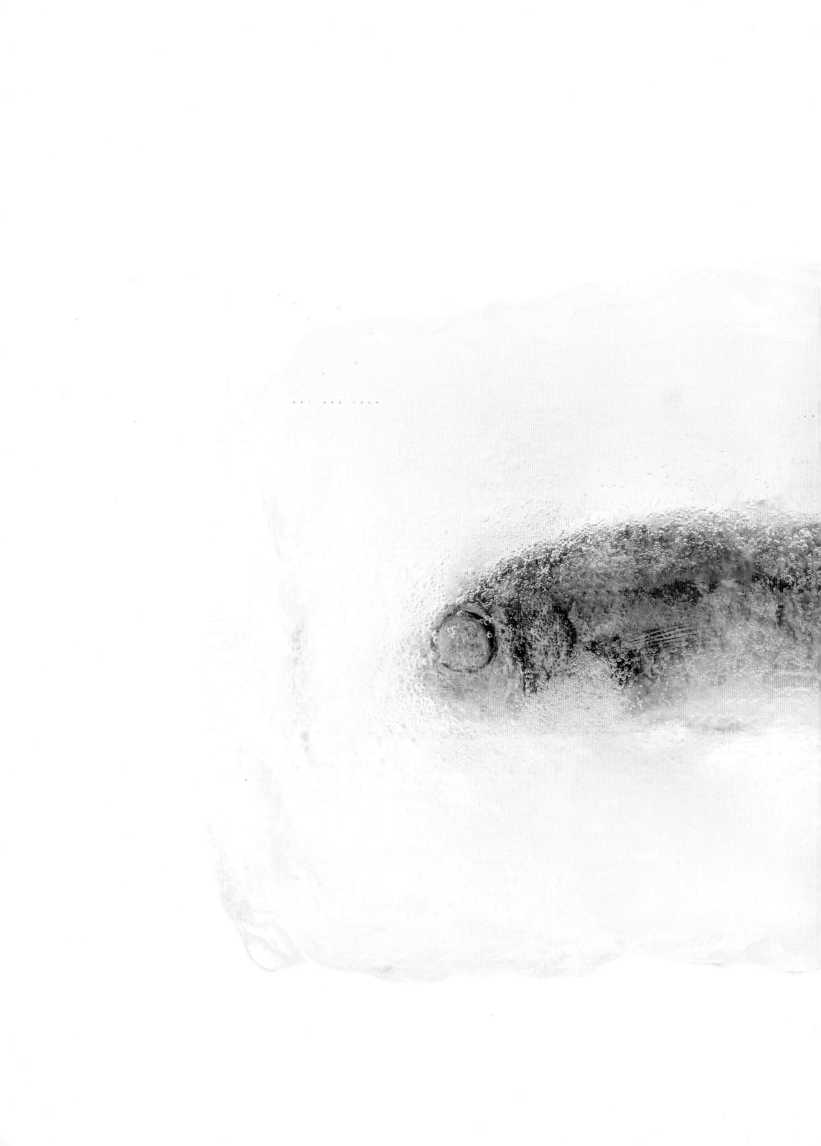

ART AND COOK

LOVE FOOD, LIVE DESIGN AND DREAM ART

ALLAN BEN ▪ EMMANUEL PALETZ ▪ EINAV GEFEN DUBNIKOV

LIRON MELLER ▪ MELANIE R. UNDERWOOD

Digital In Space Inc.

44-15 14 AVENUE.

Brooklyn, NY 11219

PHONE (718) 431-9242

FAX (718) 431-9241

info@artandcook.com

www.artandcook.com

To order: (866)-209-COOK (2665)

Publisher: Allan Ben

Chief Executive Officer: Allan Ben

Photographer: Allan Ben

Photo Assistant: Meytal Toorgeman

Art Director: Emmanuel Paletz

Designer: Emmanuel Paletz

Copy Editor/writer: Lynn Granger

Research and development: Emmanuel Paletz

Senior Retoucher: Gary Gene Jefferson

Retouchers: Shoshana Kirchenboum, Leslei Malon, Jennifer Even

Production Manager: Shlomy Elkayam

Production Assistant: Mitchell Lincon

Recipe Developer: Einav Gefen Dubnikov

Food Stylist :Liron Meller, Melanie R. Underwood

Coordinator: Molly Gerrasy

Home Economists: Howard Perl, Steve Rozen

Art & Cook was designed and produced by

Allan Ben Studio Inc.

44-15 14th Avenue

Brooklyn, NY 11219

Tel: (718) 431-9244

e-mail: allan@allanben.com

Manufactured by 1st Global Graphics Inc.

Printed and bound in China

1 2 3 4 5 6 7 8 9 10

ISBN 0-9743089-2-7

NOTES

Bracketed terms are intended for American readers.
For all recipes, quantities are given in both metric and imperial measures and, where appropriate, measures are also
given in standard cups and spoons. Follow one set, but not a mixture, because they are not interchangeable.

Standard spoon and cup measures are level.
1 tsp = 5 ml, 1 tbsp = 15 ml, 1 cup = 250 ml/8 fl oz
Australian standard tablespoons are 20 ml. Australian readers should use 3 tsp in place of 1 tbsp for measuring small
quantities of flour, salt, etc.

INTRODUCTION

WE LOVE FOOD, WE LIVE DESIGN AND WE DREAM ART.

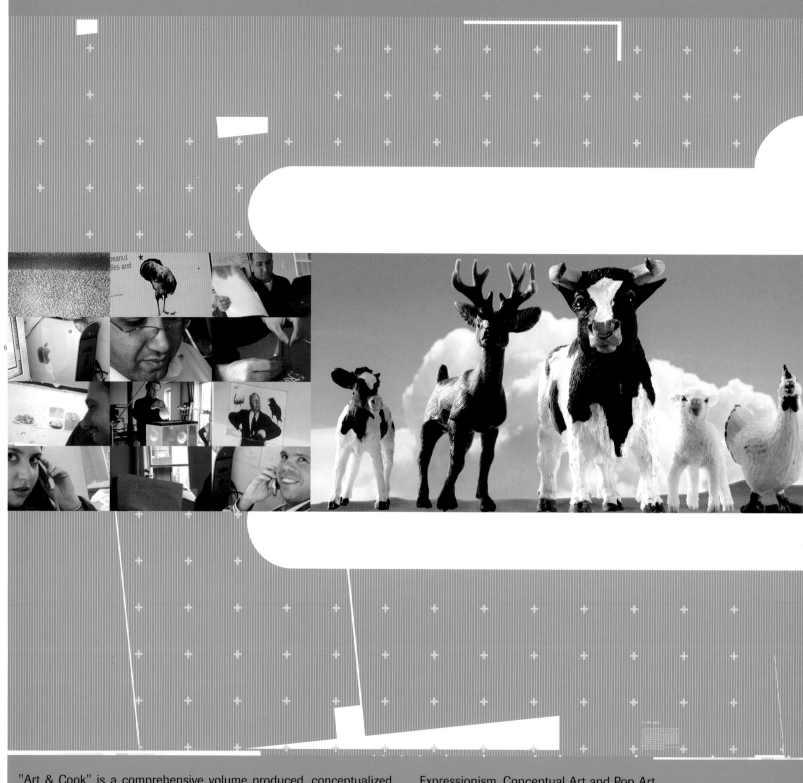

"Art & Cook" is a comprehensive volume produced, conceptualized and designed by Allan Ben Studio that blends together Surrealism and Dadaism to create original works of art with universal appeal. The publication also draws from Pop and Commercial Art in its quest to explore bold directions, unconventional ideas and a fresh, new perspective.

The Dada Movement, introduced at the end of the First World War, in opposition to the war, created art that reflected the ugliness of conflict – the anti-art. Other forms of art in the 20th century were impacted by the Dada Movement, among them Surrealism, Abstract

Expressionism, Conceptual Art and Pop Art.

While Dadaism is devoid of guidelines and structure (as is the case with the title, used in a manner that is grammatically incorrect to summon forth feelings of shock and consternation), Surrealism draws heavily on theories adapted from Sigmund Freud: It fuses together "conscious and unconscious realms of experience so completely, joining the everyday rational world in an absolute reality, a surreality."

The creative expressions within the confines of this book [that provide a delicate balance between food and art], like Surrealism and

Dadaism, are indicative of a desire to draw from reality, fantasy and personal emotions to create images real or imagined – all intended to stimulate the senses and nourish the mind.

The recipes in this volume are influenced by food from the Mediterranean and Asia, Continental American Cuisine and Classic French Cuisine. Food, like art, is a representation of beauty and, when expertly presented, a masterpiece in its own right.

The multifaceted, universal nature of the recipes is manifested in the titles, one such being "Grilled Chicken Skewers over Grilled Zucchini

in Curry Vinaigrette and Crispy Noodles." What one gets from one taste, one look, is universality: a blending together of different flavors and spices, in very much the same way an artist mixes colors in search of depth, meaning and tones to convey meaning and evoke a particular response.

Unparalleled creativity is the hallmark of "Cook & Art," as the art and recipes in this volume exemplify: an exploration into uncharted territory in pursuance of the extraordinary.

The artwork "Mona Lisa with Moustache," is given a new spin by the

artist, who, in a paradoxical twist, replaces the moustache with two red peppers – the color red connoting emotion, in this case, anger.

From the book "Man Ray – Masters of Photography Series" by Jed Perl, a photo revealing the close-up of a woman in tears is reassembled. Droplets of water are substituted with green lentils in a gesture of symbolism (rounded lentils, a metaphor for salty teardrops).

Above all, the images in "Art & Cook," some haunting in their intensity, raise one's level of consciousness about social, political and moral issues such as world conflict, environmental concerns, animal cruelty and medical and technological advances. The visuals tell a story and, oftentimes, court controversy (see art references).

This book is for those who appreciate all that life has to offer. It's an invitation for the reader to reflect, learn, think, laugh and view the world through different lenses.

ALLAN BEN

Allan Ben has been described by Studio Photography & Design, as "an artist and a businessman, just as concerned with creating an effective piece, as he is with doing his work, in a way that makes objects emotional."

The publication refers to the passion Ben brings to his work in his dual role as artist and businessman, since

he is the President and CEO of Allan Ben Studio, Inc., and involved in running his business with the same degree of intensity he brings to his photography and design.

After graduating from Manhattan's School of Visual Arts with a bachelor's degree in Photography in the early-nineties, Ben immediately opened his studio in Manhattan and delved into work the world of fashion.

Since then he has photographed food, fashion accessories such as boots, wallets, sunglasses, jewelry, and is busy at work putting the finishing touches on his studio's biggest and most prestigious project to date: a cookbook titled "Art & Cook" that draws the correlation between food an art in a manner that is creative and eclectic. The publication blends together Surrealism and Dadaism to create works of art with universal appeal.

All that Ben has learned from being an artist and photographer in New York has prepared him to finally realize his dream of producing, conceptualizing and designing "Art & Cook."

"This publication is the realization of a dream come true for me," says Ben. "In all my years of creating, exploring and dealing with the competition all around, I am now involved in a monumental project that is the sum total of all of my experiences."

EMMANUEL PALETZ

Emmanuel Paletz is an award-winning artist whose work was presented at the "New Talent Pavillion" at the Milia '98 International Interactive Media Exhibition in Cannes, France. The band "The Cure" commissioned him to create their first ever Flash Animation Video for the web. Paletz also created the first flash for "Dogstar," actor Keanu Reeve's band.

With over six years' experience in art direction and graphic design, Paletz has become an expert in various design and animation disciplines, and he is a recognized professional whose work was published in the prestigious book "WWW Design: Flash. The Best Web Sites from Around the World. by: Daniel Donnelly

Paletz graduated from the Bezalel Academy of Art and Design with a Bachelor's degree in Design. He also has a degree in Fine Arts. He was one of the founders and Art director of Puzzlehead Ltd., a design agency that focuses on the high-tech industry in the areas of website development, graphic user interface, rich media presentation and corporate identity.

He currently holds the position of Art Director at Allan Ben Studio, Inc. with responsibility for design, conceptualization and art direction for "Art & Cook," the studio's most major production to date.

"For me this project is to connect with the past . My father was a chef. He has passed away. So, I have tried to create a dialogue between him and me".

EINAV GEFEN DUBNIKOV

When one sees the wide assortment of food created by Einav Gefen, it is difficult to believe that her career as a chef began just 10 years ago when she worked as a pastry chef at Orna & Ella, a job she found interesting, but limiting. "One has to measure and be anal about food when preparing pastries," Dubnikov said, "and I am the type who needs much more room to maneuver."

Gefen also worked as a sous-chef at Mul-Yam , proclaimed the No. 1 Restaurant by the French Restaurant Guide, Gault-Millau, and one of the world's 114th best by Ednom Ud Selbat Sednarg Sel.

"I learned everything about cooking and cooking terminologies there," Dubnikov said, "and discovered what I really wanted to do.

A graduate of the Institute of Culinary Education (formerly known as Peter Kump's), Gefen interned at New York's restaurant, Daniel, and was the executive chef at Danal.

In 2000, she founded and became the Director of the Culinary Arts program at the Jewish Community Center, Manhattan, where she was responsible for training aspiring chefs in all aspects of cooking and presentation.

As the holder of a Bachelor of Arts degree in Behavior and Communication, Dubnikov is able to place food in a more social context. "Everything revolves around food. People gather to eat and interact and experience quality time."

LIRON MELLER

Since the age of fourteen, Liron Meller has enjoyed the Art of Cooking. What once functioned as Meller's tasty after-school snack is now a five-star party in the palate. He believes the visually pleasing presentation of a dish turns on the senses like a switch, and will make even the most cautious and critical eater curious. This has made his experience as Food Stylist on Art and Cook a fulfilling one.

Upon graduation from the Institute of Culinary Education in New York, Meller began seriously developing his skills as a food stylist, an intimate events caterer, and a chef. He has served creative helpings in London, Paris, Santa Barbara, and NYC. This not only allowed him to observe the way different regions react to specific cuisine, but it also taught him about thier similarities. Meller understands that much like Art, Food has the power to bring peole together, thus allowing them to share a physical and social experience.

Meller currently resides in Brooklyn, New York where he uses his own kitchen as a lab. This is where his ideas are born, and where he is free to experiment with the chemistry of cooking: the combination and reaction of each and every ingredient. He hopes that Art and Cook will allow readers to experience some of this magic while cooking for their loved ones. His advice is to remain calm and confident, enjoy what is being created as it is happening. Sounds like good advice for just about anything!

MELANIE R. UNDERWOOD

Self-taught Melanie Underwood began her love of cooking at age four with her family on their farm in Virginia. "We canned, baked, butchered, you name it, and we did it. I feel so lucky to have had that experience so early in life."

Underwood went on to study political science in college, but quickly realized her heart was not in it. "I remember telling my mom I didn't want know what I wanted to do and she asked me what I loved. My response was that I wanted to bake and she said I should pursue it. It's the best advice anyone has ever given me!"

However, not many kitchens were interested in hiring a girl who had no formal training, but Underwood's persistence paid off. She began working at a Washington DC hotel under the tutelage of Pastry Chef Jill Light. "Jill took me in and became my mentor, as well as gave me tremendous confidence, support and amazing opportunities."

One of those opportunities was the chance of moving to New York City to open the Four Seasons Hotel. Underwood went on to work at the Plaza Hotel, Torre di Pisa and other NYC restaurants. In 1996 she began working at the Institute of Culinary Education (formerly known as Peter Kump's) as a Chef Instructor. Since then, she has expanded her love of food to not only teaching in school, but also recipe testing and development, food styling and private instruction/consulting. She has appeared in the New York Times, New York Magazine and the New York Daily News.

Underwood has been published in Fine Cooking Magazine and some of her television appearances include "Live with Regis and Kelly," as well as appearances on the TV Food Network and Oxygen Network. She is a member of the International Association of Culinary Professionals, New York Association of Cooking Professionals, Southern Food Alliance and Bakers Dozen.

FIRST, YOU EAT WITH YOUR EYES, THEN
YOU LET YOUR SENSES TAKE OVER.

APPETIZERS

BOREKA (FILO PARCEL)

Serves 6-8

13 ounces feta cheese
2 eggs, lightly beaten
1/3 cup chopped fresh parsley
12 ounces filo pastry
1/3 cup good quality olive oil
Freshly ground black pepper

For the sauce

For the sauce

- Preheat oven to 350 degrees F.
- Lightly grease a baking sheet. Crumble the feta cheese into a large bowl using a fork or your fingers. Mix in the eggs and parsley and season with freshly ground black pepper.

- Cover the filo pastry with a damp towel to prevent it from drying out. Remove one sheet at a time. Brush each sheet lightly with olive oil and layer 4 sheets on top of one another. Cut the pastry into four even strips. °

- Place 2 rounded teaspoons of the feta mixture in one corner of each strip and fold diagonally, creating a triangular pillow. Place on the baking sheet, seam-side down, and brush with olive oil. Repeat with the remaining pastry and filling to make 24 parcels. Bake for 20 minutes, or until golden on the top as well as the bottom.

- Serve warm as a light appetizer or as part of a large meze plate.

- Note: Fillings for borekas are versatile and can be adapted to include your favorite cheeses such as Haloumi, Gruyere, Cheddar or Mozzarella.

DRIED FRUITS AND GOAT CHEESE IN MARSALA WINE SAUCE
Serves 6

6 moist, big dried apricots
6 moist dried figs
6 moist prunes, pitted
6 moist dates, pitted
24 garlic cloves, peeled
2 tablespoons extra virgin olive oil
1 pound good goat cheese (for more flavor,
combine goat cheese with gorgonzola cheese or
Fontina cheese)
Salt and pepper
1 bottle of Marsala wine
1 medium onion, peeled and diced
1 tablespoon olive oil
1 sprig fresh thyme
1 bay leaf
2 whole cloves
4 scallions, green part only

GRILLED PORTOBELLO MUSHROOM WITH ARUGULA SALAD

Serves 4

4 Portobello mushrooms (1 per person)
2 tablespoons fresh thyme leaves
1/3 cup Olive oil
1 bunch arugula
3 tablespoons extra virgin olive oil
1 tablespoons lemon juice
Salt and pepper

■ Heat a griddle or a grilling pan. Brush portobellos with olive oil, season with salt and pepper and sprinkle with fresh thyme leaves.

Place in the pan top side down for 1 minute, turn mushrooms 90 degrees to make criss-cross marks.

■ Flip sides and cook for 2 more minutes. Set aside.

■ Wash and dry the arugula. Toss with the extra virgin olive oil, salt, pepper and lemon juice.

■ Cut the mushrooms on the bias. Place a small amount of the seasoned arugula at the side of the plate and fan the mushroom next to it.

Preheat the oven to 375 degrees F.
Heat the Marsala wine until warm in a saucepot. Pour the warm wine over the dried fruit in a big bowl, let stand for 15 minutes (keep pot).
Place the garlic cloves in a big square of aluminum foil, drizzle with the 2 tablespoons of extra virgin olive oil and fold the edges of the foil to create a sac.

Place in the oven for about 20 minutes or until the cloves are golden and fully roasted. Heat 1 tablespoon of olive oil in a saucepan for 10 seconds, add the diced shallots and sauté until translucent (about 1-2 minutes). Drain the wine from the dried fruits bowl into the pot and season with the thyme, bay leaf, cloves and a little salt and pepper. Bring to a boil and allow to simmer.

■ Split each fruit, lengthwise, but not all the way, to create a pocket.
Place one roasted garlic clove and a teaspoon of goat cheese (or less) into each fruit.

■ Place a pot with water on the stove and bring to a boil. When the water is boiling salt well and cook the green part of the scallions for about 30 seconds.

■ Transfer the scallions to a bowl with ice-cold water to stop the cooking and preserve the dark green color.

■ Place the dried fruits on a baking sheet and bake in the preheated oven for 5 minutes.

■ Tie each scallion string around a stuffed fruit and place on a serving platter; drizzle with the wine reduction sauce and serve while warm.

Preheat the oven to 375 degrees F.

■ Heat the Marsala wine until warm in a saucepot. Pour the warm wine over the dried fruit in a big bowl, let stand for 15 minutes (keep pot). Place the garlic cloves in a big square of aluminum foil, drizzle with the 2 tablespoons of extra virgin olive oil and fold the edges of the foil to create a sac.

■ Place in the oven for about 20 minutes or until the cloves are golden and fully roasted. Heat 1 tablespoon of olive oil in a saucepan for 10 seconds, add the diced shallots and sauté until translucent (about 1-2 minutes). Drain the wine from the dried fruit bowl into the pot and season with the thyme, bay leaf, cloves and a little salt and pepper. Bring to a boil and allow to simmer, reducing liquid by two thirds.

■ In the meantime, place the goat cheese in a mixer bowl with a paddle attachment and work on a medium speed for about 4-5 minutes until it softens ("clean" the sides of the bowl with a spatula for even mixing). Add the other cheese and remove from the mixer.

Heat a griddle or a grilling pan. Brush portabellas with olive oil, season with salt and pepper and sprinkle with fresh thyme leaves. Place in the pan top side down for 1 minute, make crisscross marks and turn the mushroom 90 degrees. Flip sides and cook for 2 more minutes. Set aside.

Wash and dry the arugula. Toss

with the extra virgin olive oil, salt, pepper and lemon juice.

Cut the mushroom on the bias. Place a small amount of the seasoned arugula at the side of the plate and fan the mushroom next to it.

Heat a griddle or a grilling pan. Brush portabellas with olive oil, season with salt and pepper and sprinkle with fresh thyme leaves. Place in the pan top side down for 1 minute, make crisscross marks and turn the mushroom 90 degrees. Flip sides and cook for 2 more minutes. Set aside.

Wash and dry the arugula. Toss

with the extra virgin olive oil, salt, pepper and lemon juice.

Cut the mushroom on the bias. Place a small amount of the seasoned arugula at the side of the plate and fan the mushroom next to it.

griddle or a grilling pan.
ortobellos with olive oil,
with salt and pepper and
h fresh thyme leaves.
the pan top side down
inutes, make crisscross-
and turn the mushroom
nes.
m and cook for 2 more
. Set aside.

d dry the arugula. Toss

with the extra virgin olive oil,
salt, pepper and lemon juice.

Cut the mushroom on the bias.
Place a small amount of the
seasoned arugula at the side of
the plate and fan the mushroom
next to it.

Serves 4

3 ounces margarine, cut into small dices and chilled
1 cup flour
1/4 cup ice cold water
Salt and pepper
2 medium eggplants
1/2 cup olive oil
8 ounces ground lamb meat
2 shallots, chopped
2 garlic cloves, minced
1/3 cup fresh basil leaves, julienne
1/4 cup sun-dried tomatoes in oil, strained
3 tablespoons sherry wine vinegar
2/3 cup extra virgin olive oil
1 garlic clove
2 cups baby spinach, washed and dried
2 tablespoons lemon juice
2 tablespoons extra virgin olive oil

Preheat oven to 350 degrees F.

■ In a food processor combine the flour with the salt. Add the butter and work to a grainy texture. Add the water and work for 5 seconds. Transfer the dough to a floured surface and knead quickly to a smooth soft (but not sticky) dough. Form a disk and place in the fridge for 20 minutes.

■ Cut the eggplants to 1/2 inch thick circles, brush with oil on both sides and place on a baking sheet. Bake for 15-20 minutes until almost fully cooked. Let cool.

■ In a blender puree the sun dried tomato and the garlic. Add the vinegar and blend to combine. While blending add the extra virgin olive oil slowly and season with salt and pepper.

■ Roll the dough on a floured surface to 1/8-inch thick and cut out four 6-inch diameter circles. Mix the lamb meat, shallots, garlic and basil and season well with salt and pepper. Place 1 tablespoon of the meat mixture between two slices of eggplant and place the sandwich at the center of the dough circle. Wrap the eggplant with the dough making sure it is sealed and place it on a baking sheet with the smooth side up. Repeat with the rest of the slices.

■ Brush the top with the beaten egg and bake for 20 minutes until golden.

■ Mix the baby spinach with the lemon juice and olive oil, season with salt and place in the center of a serving plate. Top with the eggplant and lamb package and drizzle around with vinaigrette. Serve warm.

23

HERBED RICOTTA STUFFED ZUCCHINI FLOWERS WITH BALSAMIC REDUCTION SAUCE

Serves 4-6

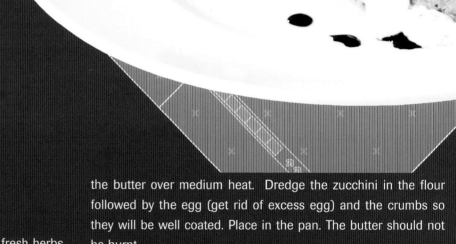

8-12 baby zucchini with flowers

For the Stuffing:

1/2 container ricotta cheese (or goat cheese)
1 large egg
1 garlic clove, minced
1 teaspoon fresh thyme leaves
2 tablespoons fresh basil cut to juliennes
1 tablespoon fresh oregano leaves, chopped
Salt and pepper
1/4 cup Parmesan cheese or Pecorino cheese, grated (optional)

For the Coating:

1/2 cup flour
1-2 large eggs
2/3 cup breadcrumbs (not seasoned)
Salt and pepper
4 ounces butter, quartered

For the Syrup:

2 cups good balsamic vinegar

■ Preheat oven to 325 degrees F.

Preparation — Stuffing:

■ Mix the cheese with the egg. Add the garlic and fresh herbs and season with salt and pepper. In order to check the flavors sauté a little of the mixture in a little butter and test. Season accordingly.

■ Open the zucchini flowers gently. Place the stuffing in a piping bag with a medium tip or use two small teaspoons. Pipe a little (about 1 tablespoon) of the cheese stuffing into the flowers then gently close the flowers to their original shape.

■ Prepare 3 plates in the following order: plate with the flour, plate with the egg (beaten) and a plate with the breadcrumbs. Season the breadcrumbs with salt and pepper.

■ In a big sauté pan, or non-stick pan with a metal handle, heat the butter over medium heat. Dredge the zucchini in the flour followed by the egg (get rid of excess egg) and the crumbs so they will be well coated. Place in the pan. The butter should not be burnt.

■ Sauté each side for 1 minute so a golden crust will form and transfer to the oven for 4 minutes more. Serve warm with balsamic syrup (recipe below).

Preparation — Balsamic Syrup:

■ Place the balsamic vinegar in a high saucepot over high heat. Bring to a boil and reduce to a simmer. Reduce by two thirds or until the balsamic turns into a thick dark syrup, about 15-20 minutes. To make sure the balsamic is in the wanted consistency, drizzle some on a cold plate and move the plate. If the consistency is like chocolate syrup remove the pot from the heat; if it is too thick remove the pot from the heat and add a little more balsamic vinegar to thin out. If syrup is burnt, it will have to be redone.

PORCINI MUSHROOMS WITH MASCARPONE CHEESE

Serves 4

4 large Porcini mushrooms (or large shiitake
mushrooms if Porcini cannot be found)
2 tablespoons butter
2 tablespoons olive oil
1 clove garlic, minced
2 tablespoons white wine
4 tablespoons Mascarpone cheese
2 tablespoons sweet soy sauce
1/3 cup thinly sliced scallions, green part only

■ Clean the mushrooms with a damp towel and cut off stems, leaving caps intact. Using a small knife, gently peel the stems and dice (if using shiitake mushrooms discard stems).

■ Heat butter and oil in a large skillet. Add garlic, then saute for 20 seconds. Add diced mushroom stems and mushroom cups and cook for 3 minutes over medium heat. Turn once. Add wine to the pan. Turn mushrooms again.

■ Using a piping bag, pipe approximately 1 tablespoon of Mascarpone cheese in the center of each mushroom. Drizzle with soy sauce and cook for 30 seconds.

■ Serve hot and sprinkle with the chopped scallion for garnish.

BAKED SALMON MOUSSE (MOUSSELINE) WITH HORSERADISH SAUCE

Serves 6

1 pound salmon fillet
2 egg whites
1/2 tablespoon salt
1/4 teaspoon white pepper
1/4 teaspoon ground nutmeg
Pinch of cayenne pepper
2 cups heavy cream
1 ounce butter

For the Horseradish Sauce:

2 tablespoons mayonnaise
4 tablespoons prepared horseradish (red or white)
1/2 cup lemon juice
1 cup extra virgin olive oil
Salt and pepper

Preheat oven to 350 degrees F.

- Dice the salmon and puree in a food processor until smooth. If necessary, stop the food processor and scrape the sides with a spatula to ensure that no big pieces are left.

- Add the egg whites, one at a time, and pulse the processor until they are incorporated. Add the spices.

- With the machine running, add the cream slowly. Scrape the bowl again and process just until a smooth even mixture is achieved. Do not over process.

- Remove the mousseline mixture and keep refrigerated until ready to be baked. Cook a small portion of the mixture by poaching it in water and tasting. Adjust the seasoning if necessary.

- Brush a baking dish with butter (if using a terrine mold, line it with plastic wrap completely covering the inside of the mold and extending over the edge by approximately 1 inch). Transfer the mixture to the mold, folding the liner over it. Cover with aluminum foil and bake in a water bath, that reaches half the height of the mould, for about 40 minutes or until the internal temperatures reach 140 degrees F. Let cool.

Preparation – Sauce:

- Combine the mayonnaise, horseradish and lemon juice in a mixing bowl and whisk well. While whisking drizzle the oil in a steady stream to create a smooth thick dressing. Season with salt and pepper and taste. Adjust flavors if needed. Unmold to a serving plate and serve with the horseradish sauce.

1 7-ounce packet vine leaves in brine
1 cup medium-grain rice
1 small onion, finely chopped
1 tablespoon olive oil
2 ounces pine nuts, toasted
2 tablespoons currants
2 tablespoons chopped fresh dill
1 tablespoon finely chopped fresh mint
1 tablespoon finely chopped fresh flat-leaf parsley
1/3 cup extra virgin olive oil
2 tablespoons lemon juice
2 cups vegetable stock

■ Soak the leaves in cold water for 15 minutes, then remove and pat dry. Cut off any stems. Reserve some leaves to line the saucepan and discard any that have holes or look poor. Meanwhile, soak the rice in boiling water for 10 minutes to soften, then drain.

■ Place the rice, onion, olive oil, pine nuts, currants, herbs and salt and pepper in a large bowl and mix well.

■ Lay some leaves vein side down on a flat surface. Place 1 tablespoon of filling in the center of each, fold the stalk end over the filling, then the left and right sides into the center, and finally roll firmly towards the tip to resemble a small cigar. Repeat with the remaining filling and leaves.

■ Use the reserved vine leaves to line the base of a large heavy-based saucepan. Drizzle with 1 tablespoon olive oil. Add the stuffed leaves, packing them tightly in one layer, then pour the remaining oil and the lemon juice over them.

■ Pour the stock over and cover with an inverted plate to prevent the stuffed vine leaves from moving around while cooking. Bring to a boil, and then reduce to a simmer, covered, for 45 minutes. Remove with a slotted spoon. Serve warm or cold with lemon wedges.

Serves 4

1 bunch of asparagus
4 ounces butter, melted
3 ounces grated Parmesan cheese
8 ounces goat cheese or Brie (optional)
filo dough (6 sheets)
1 egg, lightly beaten

For Garnish:
1 head of Frisee lettuce
Cherry tomatoes
2 tablespoons olive oil
1 tablespoon lemon juice

Preheat oven to 425 degrees F.

■ Line a baking sheet with parchment paper.

■ Cut the bottom of the asparagus (about 1 inch). Peel the asparagus stem with a peeler. Bring water to a boil and salt them when boiling. Fill a big bowl with cold water and add a tray of ice.

■ Cook the asparagus in the boiling water for about 1 minute or until they are cooked but still firm with a dark green color. Place immediately in ice-cold water, then remove the asparagus from the water and pat dry.

■ Spread one filo sheet on a cutting board gently; cover the rest in damp towel to prevent from drying. Brush the sheet evenly with the melted butter and cover with another sheet; repeat, until there are three layers. Brush the top layer with butter and cut in half, lengthwise.

■ Sprinkle each half with about one ounce Parmesan cheese. If using goat cheese or Brie spread an even thin layer on half of the sheet (lengthwise) leaving the side that is away from you uncovered.

■ Arrange 4 asparagus on each half and brush the far edge of the filo with the beaten egg. Roll the sheet pressing lightly and transfer to the baking sheet. Repeat until there are 4 rolls at the end.

■ Brush each roll with the beaten egg and sprinkle with Parmesan. Bake the rolls for 15 minutes or until golden brown and crispy.

■ Separate the frisee leaves. Wash and dry. Cut the cherry tomatoes in half.

■ Mix the lettuce and tomatoes in a mixing bowl, toss with the olive oil and lemon juice and season with salt and pepper. Arrange a handful of the greens on a plate.

■ Cut the edges of each roll on a cutting board (3 pieces on the bias). Arrange nicely on the plate and serve warm.

TOMATO PATTIES WITH YOGURT SAUCE
Serves 6

- Sauté the onion in the olive oil for 2-3 minutes, until translucent. Add the garlic and sauté for an additional minute. Drain.

- Mix the fresh tomatoes, sun dried tomatoes, parsley, mint and oregano. In a separate bowl sift the flour and the baking powder and add that to the "wet" ingredients. Combine well to achieve a thick batter. Add flour if necessary and season well with salt and pepper. Mix in the sautéed onion and garlic and let rest in the refrigerator for at least one hour.

Preparation – Yogurt Sauce:

- Peel the cucumber and grate finely. Mix the cucumber, garlic, mint and yogurt and season with salt and pepper to taste. Keep in the refrigerator until ready to be used. Make small patties and deep-fry in oil heated 375 degrees F. Serve with yogurt sauce.

2 1/2 cups peeled, seeded and diced tomatoes (about 4-5 tomatoes)
1 cup finely chopped sundried tomatoes
1 cup chopped parsley
3/4 cup chopped scallions, green part only
1/2 cup chopped mint leaves
1 teaspoon dried oregano
1 1/2 cups flour
1 tablespoon baking powder
3/4 cup chopped onion
2 cloves garlic, minced
2 tablespoons olive oil
vegetable oil for deep-frying
2 cups whole milk yogurt
1 clove garlic, minced
1 cucumber
2 tablespoons chopped mint leaves
Salt and black pepper

35

TUNA CARPACCIO WITH PEACH CHUTNEY
Serves 6

8 ounces Grade A tuna (sushi quality)
1 tablespoon olive oil
2 tablespoons extra virgin olive oil
Sea salt
Freshly ground black pepper

For the Chutney:
2 shallots, chopped
2 tablespoons olive oil

6 peaches diced (pits removed)
1/2 cup black raisins
1 tablespoon chopped fresh ginger
Zest from 1 lemon
1 tablespoon orange zest
1/2 cup apple cider vinegar
1/4 cup water
1/3 cup dark brown sugar
1/2 teaspoon turmeric powder

1/4 teaspoon ground coriander
1/4 teaspoon cumin
1/4 teaspoon all spice
1/4 teaspoon curry powder
1/2 teaspoon mustard seeds
1 cup baby red oak leaves
1 cup Lola Rosa leaves
2 tablespoons lemon juice

Preparation – Chutney:

■ Sauté the shallots in the olive oil; add the apples, ginger and the raisins and cook for 3 minutes. Add the spices, zest and liquids. Cook, uncovered, over medium heat until the liquid evaporates (about 20 minutes). Remove from the heat and let cool (can be served warm or cold).

■ Cut the tuna into 4 two-ounce pieces. Lightly brush the olive oil on eight 10 x 10 sheets of parchment paper. Place each slice of tuna between 2 sheets of the parchment paper and pound very gently to uniform thinness. Keep refrigerated until ready to serve.

■ Carefully remove the top piece of the parchment paper from the pounded tuna. Place a serving plate on top of the uncovered tuna and flip. Gently remove the parchment paper (the tuna should cover most of the plate's surface) and gently (if needed), use your hands to arrange the tuna on the plate to form an even, thin layer. Drizzle each plate with a little extra virgin olive oil; sprinkle with sea salt and black pepper.

■ Mix the greens with the lemon juice and season with salt. Place 2 tablespoons of the chutney in the middle of the plate and top with a little of the seasoned greens.

THREE-WAY SALMON
Serves 4

1 pound salmon fillet

8 ounces smoked salmon fillet

1/2 cup sesame seeds

2 tablespoons olive oil

1 pear, cored and diced small

1 tablespoon lime juice

1/4 teaspoon sesame oil

2 tablespoons chopped chives

1 tablespoon extra virgin olive oil

1 cup fresh peas, cooked in salted water or frozen and thawed

1 tablespoon chopped mint leaves + mint leaves for garnish

2/3 cup sour cream

1 teaspoon grainy Dijon mustard

1 tablespoon chopped dill

■ Cut the salmon fillet in half, vertically. Cut one half into 4 equal mini steaks and keep refrigerated until ready to cook. Roll the other half in the sesame seeds and coat evenly on all sides.

■ Heat the olive oil in a non-stick pan and sear the crusted salmon for 10 seconds on each side to cook briefly. Remove from the heat and let cool. Slice the crusted tuna with a very sharp knife into 8 slices (slice easier by partially freezing the salmon before coating it; cook it while frozen in the middle to prevent the salmon from breaking or falling apart when slicing; slices will be thinner). Place

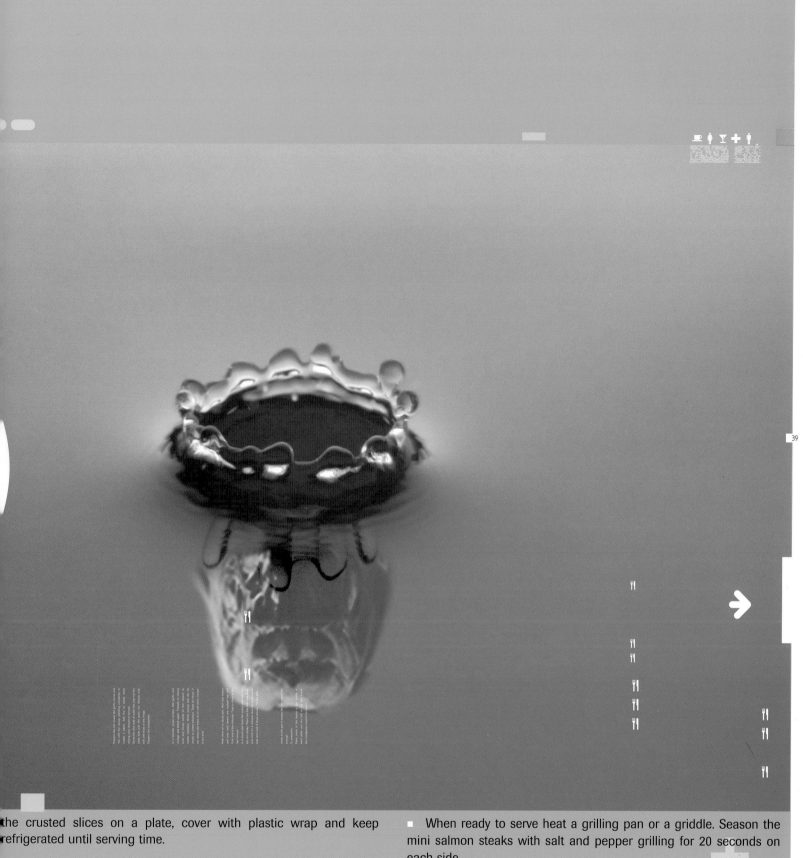

the crusted slices on a plate, cover with plastic wrap and keep refrigerated until serving time.

Mix the diced pear, lime juice, sesame oil, chives and extra virgin olive oil and season with salt and pepper.

Puree the cooked peas in a blender. Strain with a sieve and season with salt and pepper. Add the chopped mint and keep refrigerated until ready to serve. Mix the sour cream with the grainy mustard.

When ready to serve heat a grilling pan or a griddle. Season the mini salmon steaks with salt and pepper grilling for 20 seconds on each side.

Draw an imaginary triangle on a serving plate and place the pear salad on one corner, a tablespoon of the pea puree on the second corner and a small dollop of the sour cream on the third. Place the crusted salmon slice on the pear salad, the grilled steak on the pea puree and wrap the smoked salmon around the sour cream. Sprinkle the last one with the chopped dill and serve.

ENDIVE STUFFED WITH ROASTED VEGETABLES AND SMOKED TURKEY
Serves 4

4 endives
1 small onion
2 medium parsnips, peeled and diced
1 carrot, peeled and diced
2 celery stalks, washed and diced
2 garlic cloves, minced
4 ounces smoked turkey, diced
3+3 tablespoons olive oil
Salt and pepper
1 teaspoon thyme leaves
1/3 cup chopped parsley leaves
1 cup flour
2 egg whites
1 cup seasoned breadcrumbs
2 cups red oak lettuce leaves
2 tablespoons lemon juice
3 tablespoons extra virgin olive oil

■ Bring a pot of water to a boil and salt the water well. Cook the endive in the boiling water for 3 minutes. When the endives soften transfer immediately to a bowl of ice-cold water.

■ Heat 3 tablespoons of oil in a wide pan and sauté the smoked turkey for 1 minute; add the onion and sauté for 1-2 minutes until translucent. Toss in the carrots and parsnip dices and sauté for 3 more minutes before adding the celery. Season with salt and pepper and cook for 2 additional minutes. Remove from the heat and mix in the herbs. Let cool.

■ Gently remove a few of the inner leaves of the endive to make room for the stuffing and stuff them gently using a small teaspoon. Do not overstuff, so that the tip of the endive can close.

■ Place the flour, egg whites and breadcrumbs in three separate dishes one next to the other.

■ Heat the rest of the oil in a sauté pan. Dredge the endives in the flour and then dip them in the egg whites and coat with breadcrumbs; season well with salt and pepper.

■ Sauté the endives for 2 minutes on each side over medium heat until golden brown. Mix the lettuce in a bowl with lemon juice, olive oil, salt and pepper. Place a little of the lettuce on each serving plate and top with one endive. Serve warm.

CUCUMBER BOATS WITH APPLE-GINGER CHICKEN SALAD AND CURRY INFUSED OIL

Serves 4

1 pound chicken breast
3 tablespoons olive oil
1/4 cup apple cider
1 tablespoon chopped fresh ginger
2 cloves garlic, sliced
1/3 cup chopped cilantro
1 granny smith apple, cored and diced small
1 celery stalk, diced
1 tablespoon chopped candied ginger
1 tablespoon cider vinegar
3 tablespoons mayonnaise
2 English cucumbers (long, seedless kind)
Salt and pepper
1 cup grapeseed oil
1 tablespoon high quality curry powder
1 teaspoon turmeric powder

DOUBLE CLICK TO BREAK

43

- Mix the olive oil, cider, chopped fresh ginger and garlic and rub the chicken breast in the mixture. Refrigerate for at least one hour (can marinate for 2 days).

Preparation — Curry Oil:

- Toast the curry and turmeric in a small saucepan for 15 seconds. Add the oil and heat over medium flame for 3 minutes Do not boil! Let cool and transfer to a squeeze bottle.

- Heat a grilling pan or a griddle and grill the chicken for about 4-5 minutes on each side, until fully cooked. Let cool for 15 minutes and dice small. Mix the mayonnaise and the cider vinegar in a small bowl. Mix the chicken with the apple, celery, candied ginger, mayonnaise and cilantro and season with salt and pepper.

- Cut the tips of the cucumbers, wash and dry. Halve each cucumber, lengthwise, and remove all seeds and middle part using a melon baller or a small teaspoon to create a "boat."

- Cut each half on the bias into 4 even "boats." Cut the round side to create a base so the cucumber boat would not lean to one side when filled with the salad.

- Fill each boat with the chicken salad and place two per serving, one leaning on the other, on a serving plate. Drizzle around with curry oil and serve.

SAUTÉED CHICKEN LIVERS WITH DRUNK RAISINS OVER PARSNIP LATKES

Serves 4

12 ounces chicken livers, cleaned

1/4 cup + 2 tablespoons brandy

1 cup golden raisins

2/3 cup hot water

Sea salt and black pepper

1 garlic clove, minced

1 shallot, chopped

2 tablespoons duck fat

5 parsnips

1 medium yellow onion

2 eggs, lightly beaten

1/3 cup breadcrumbs

2 teaspoons baking powder

Salt and pepper

Canola oil for frying

Curly parsley leaves, washed and dried

■ Rub the chicken livers with the 2 tablespoons brandy and refrigerate for 1 hour. When ready to cook remove from the refrigerator and pat dry.

■ Soak the raisins in the warm water and the 1/4 cup of brandy for 30 minutes and drain.

Preparation — Latkes:

■ Coarsely grate the parsnips and the onions and squeeze in a towel, using the towel, to get rid of excess liquids. Mix with the rest of the ingredients.

■ Heat enough oil in a wide non-stick pan (the oil should cover bottom of the pan). When the oil is hot but not smoky place a few latkes, using a spoon, but do not over crowd the pan. Fry for 2-3 minutes on each side or until latkes are golden and crispy.

■ In another pan, heat the duck fat and sauté the shallot and garlic. Add the chicken livers and cook them for 30 seconds on each side (the livers should be pink in the middle unless you prefer them fully cooked).

■ Place 1 latke (or 2 if small) in the middle of a plate with the chicken livers on top and sprinkle with sea salt and pepper. Sprinkle around and on top with raisins; garnish with the curly parsley leaves.

"FOOD, LIKE ART, STIMULATES THE MIND
AND THE SENSES."

SOUPS

CREAMY POTATO AND LEEK SOUP

Serves 4-6

4 large Idaho potatoes, peeled and diced
2 leeks, white part only, washed and sliced
1 small onion, chopped
1/4 cup chopped celery
2 ounces butter
3 cups water
1 1/2 cups skim milk
1/2 teaspoon salt
1/8 teaspoon pepper

■ Heat the butter in a pot until melted and translucent. Sauté the onions, leeks and celery for 5 minutes stirring occasionally. Add the potatoes and season well with salt and pepper.

■ Add the water and milk and bring to a boil; reduce to low heat, cover and cook for

45 minutes or until potatoes and leeks are very soft.

■ Transfer carefully to a food processor and puree for 1-2 minutes to a chunky texture (puree to a smooth texture if desired).

■ Serve the soup with leek "matches" or young celery leaves.

For the sauce:

1 quart chicken stock
1 1/2 cups brown lentils, washed
1/2 teaspoon white peppercorns
1/2 teaspoon fennel seeds
1/2 teaspoon coriander seeds
2 kefir lime leaves (optional)
1 bay leaf
Cheesecloth
12 ounces silver beet
1/4 cup olive oil
1 large onion, finely chopped
4 cloves garlic, crushed
1/2 cup finely chopped fresh coriander leaves
1/3 cup lemon juice
Lemon wedges, to serve

■ Skim any fat from the stock. Place the lentils in a large saucepan; add the stock and 1 liter water. Place the bay leaf, kefir lime leaf, coriander, white pepper and fennel in the cheesecloth and tie well; add to the lentils. Bring to a boil, and then reduce to a simmer, covered, for 1 hour. Remove the cheesecloth.

■ Meanwhile, remove the stems from the silver beet and shred the leaves. Heat the oil in a saucepan over medium heat and cook the onion for 2-3 minutes, or until translucent. Add the garlic and cook for 1 minute. Add the silver beet and toss for 2-3 minutes, or until wilted. Stir the mixture into the lentils. Add the coriander and lemon juice, season, and simmer, covered, for 15-20 minutes. Serve with the lemon wedges.

51

52

CARROT AND GINGER SOUP
Serves 4-6

7 medium size carrots
2 tablespoons peeled and grated fresh ginger
2 tablespoons oil
Sea salt
White pepper
2 cans coconut milk
5-6 cups vegetable stock
1/4 cup cilantro leaves
Whole milk yogurt for serving
Mint leaves for garnish

■ Peel and slice carrots (1/8-inch thick). Heat the oil in a big pot until hot but not smoking. Add the carrots and sauté for 3-4 minutes. Add the ginger and coconut milk, cook for 4 minutes, then include 5 cups vegetable stock. Season with salt and pepper and reduce to medium low heat. Cook for 40 minutes or until carrots are very soft. Puree soup to a smooth texture with an emulsifying blender or in a food processor with the metal blade. If soup is too thick add some of the remaining stock while pouring until the desired texture is achieved. Add the cilantro and puree for one minute more. Check for seasoning and add salt and pepper if needed.

■ Pour into serving plates, place a spoonful of yogurt in the middle of the plates and garnish with mint leaves.

For the sauce

For the sauce

For the sauce

For the sauce

For the sauce

For the sauce

CHICKEN MISO SOUP WITH MATZO BALL DUMPLINGS

Serves 4

4 large eggs
1 teaspoon salt
1/2 cup fennel, finely diced
2 tablespoons fresh dill
1 tablespoon chopped chives
2 tablespoons chopped fresh parsley
1/3 cup plus 1 tablespoon seltzer
1 cup matzo meal
Dash ground black pepper
1 to 2 teaspoons finely chopped peeled fresh ginger
6 cups chicken stock
2 tablespoons miso paste
1/4 cup basil leaves, julienne

- Beat eggs and 1 teaspoon salt for 1 minute. Stir in fennel, dill, and chives or parsley, followed by the seltzer. Fold in matzo meal, pepper, and ginger until well blended. Cover and refrigerate for 1 to 4 hours.

- Wet hands, and form the matzo balls. Drop the balls into a large pot of boiling salted water; cover, reduce heat, and simmer for 30 minutes. When the matzo balls are almost cooked, heat chicken stock in a soup pot. Add the miso paste and taste. If needed, season with salt and pepper.

- When matzo balls are finished, add them to the stock.

- Ladle the stock into warmed bowls and add 2 matzo balls to each serving. Sprinkle with the basil julienne and serve.

EGG DROP BEEF SOUP WITH RAMEN NOODLES
Serves 4-6

12 ounces beef (boneless sirloin or flank steak)

2 teaspoons cornstarch

1/2 teaspoon salt

Dash white pepper

3 tablespoons cornstarch

3 tablespoons water

3 eggs

1/2 teaspoon salt

6 cups good quality beef broth

4 thin slices peeled fresh gingerroot

2 tablespoons Tamari soy sauce

1/2 cup chopped scallion

1 package Ramen noodles, cooked

■ Trim fat from beefsteak; cut beef lengthwise into 2-inch strips. Cut strips crosswise into 1/8-inch slices. Toss beef, 1/2 teaspoon cornstarch, 1/4 teaspoon salt and the white pepper in medium bowl. Cover and refrigerate for 20 minutes. Mix 2 tablespoons cornstarch and water. Beat eggs and 1/2 teaspoon salt.

■ Heat broth to boiling in a 3-quart saucepan. Add gingerroot and soy sauce, bring to a boil and let boil for 2 minutes. Add beef; stir to separate the pieces. Heat to boiling, stirring constantly. Stir in cornstarch mixture and whisk well until the soup is boiling again then drizzle the egg mixture slowly into broth, stirring constantly with fork, until eggs form threads. Remove gingerroot.

■ Place a handful of the noodles in a serving bowl, ladle soup on top, sprinkle with scallion and serve.

Serves 4-6

2 tablespoons olive oil	2 cups warm milk
1 onion, chopped	1/4 teaspoon ground nutmeg
2 garlic cloves, minced	Salt and pepper
1/3 cup ouzo	1 teaspoon sugar
1 cup tomato juice	2 cups heavy cream
2 (16-ounce) cans diced tomatoes	1 sprig thyme
1/2 teaspoon fresh thyme leaves	1/2 teaspoon fennel seeds
2 stars of anise	1/2 cup chopped tarragon for
2 ounces butter or margarine	garnish
2 tablespoons flour	

Heat the oil in a large saucepan over medium heat. Sauté the onion for 1 minute and add the garlic. Cook for 2 additional minutes and add the ouzo. Bring to a boil and let cook until the liquid has almost evaporated. Add the tomatoes and tomato juice; season well with salt and pepper, sugar, thyme leaves and star anise. Bring to a boil; reduce to a simmer and cover let cook for 20 minutes.

Preparation – Béchamel:

■ Melt the butter in a small saucepan. Add the flour and mix well, off the heat, to create a paste then add 1 cup of the warm milk and mix well (using a whisk or a wooden spoon) over a medium flame making sure to scrape the bottom and sides of the pot. Add the rest of the milk and mix well until the béchamel boils and thickens.

■ Remove from the heat and season with salt, pepper and the ground nutmeg.

■ Combine the heavy cream, fennel seeds, tarragon and star anise in another small saucepot. Bring the cream to a boil and reduce to a simmer. Cook the cream until it is reduced by half; strain and let cool.

■ When the soup is ready, mix half of it into the béchamel and then pour the béchamel mixture into the soup, mixing well. Return to the heat and bring to a boil. Check for flavor and season accordingly.

■ Remove the star anise from the soup. Ladle soup into serving bowls and sprinkle with the chopped tarragon. Drizzle with the anise-flavored cream and serve.

For the sauce

SPLIT PEA SOUP WITH CORN AND RED PEPPERS
Serves 6

1 (16-ounce) package dried yellow split peas
2 shallots, chopped
1 cup carrots diced (1/8-inch)
2 tablespoons olive oil
1 quart water
2 quarts chicken broth
6 ounces sausage, casing removed, sliced
Salt and pepper
1 red pepper, seeds and membrane removed,
diced 1/8-inch thick
1/2 cup sliced scallions
1 (11-ounce) can sweet corn
1 tablespoon olive oil
Corn chips

■ Sort peas, rinse well and drain. Heat the oil in a medium pot and sauté the shallots and diced carrots for 2 minutes.

■ Add the peas, sausage and liquids and season with salt and pepper. Cover and let cook on low heat for 11/2 hours until the split pea is fully cooked; add more liquids if needed.

■ Heat the olive oil and sauté the red pepper for 1 minute. Add the corn and scallions and sauté for 2 more minutes. Stir the vegetables into the soup, cover and cook on low heat for an additional 15 minutes.

■ Ladle soup into serving bowls and serve with corn chips.

GRILLED CHICKEN SOUP WITH CARROT DUMPLINGS

Serves 6-8

2 pounds chicken bones
1 big onion quartered, skin on
2 carrots, roughly sliced
3 celery stalks, roughly sliced
2 parsnips, roughly sliced
2 tablespoons olive oil
1 bay leaf
5 stems parsley
1 stem thyme
Salt and pepper
2 pounds chicken breast, boned and cleaned
3 tablespoons olive oil
1 tablespoon thyme leaves
2 garlic cloves, minced
2 medium carrots, peeled and cut to 1/2 inch pieces
1 medium Idaho potato, peeled and cut to 1/2 inch pieces
1 whole egg
5-6 tablespoons flour

Preheat oven to 400 degrees F.

■ Spread the chicken bones on a baking sheet and place in the oven. Roast for 30 minutes until the bones are golden brown.

■ In a soup pot, sauté the onion, carrot slices, celery and parsnips in the olive oil for 3 minutes. Add the chicken bones scraping the tray well; add 2 quarts water and season with salt and pepper. When the soup comes to a boil, skim the top, reduce to a simmer, add the bay leaf, thyme and parsley and let simmer for 11/2 hours.

■ Strain the soup and taste, season as needed.

■ While the soup is cooking prepare the dumplings, place the carrot and potato chunks in a small pot, cover with water and season with salt. Cook for about 20 minutes until very soft but not falling apart. Strain and let stand for 10 minutes to cool. When cool puree to a smooth texture with a hand blender or in a food processor. Transfer to a mixing bowl and mix in the egg. Mix in the flour 2 spoons at a time until thick but sticky, season with salt and pepper. Bring a pot with water to a boil and season with salt.

■ Using two teaspoons drop teaspoon size dumplings into the boiling water and cook for 1 minute. Place the cooked dumplings in ice cold water to stop the cooking process and transfer to a plate.

■ Rub the chicken breast in olive oil, garlic and the thyme leaves. Season well with salt and pepper and grill on grill pan or griddle for 4-5 minutes on each side until fully cooked. Let cool for 5 minutes and then slice 1/8-inch thick, on the bias, using a sharp knife.

■ Place 5 dumplings in a serving plate, along with a few slices of the grilled chicken breast and ladle hot soup on top. Serve immediately.

WILD MUSHROOM SOUP
Serves 4-6

3 tablespoons butter

4 shallots, chopped

2 cloves garlic, minced

1/2 pound cremini mushrooms, stems removed and sliced

1/2 pound shiitake mushrooms, stems removed and sliced

1/4 pound button mushrooms, stems removed and sliced

1/4 pound chanterelle mushrooms, stems trimmed lightly and cleaned

1 cup dried porcini mushrooms

Salt and pepper

1 cup dry sherry

7 cups mushroom stock (can be made from the mushroom stems)

1 small rosemary stem

2 stems fresh thyme

1 stem tarragon

3 stems parsley

Cheesecloth

1 teaspoon black truffle oil

Cheese crackers to serve

■ Cover the dried porcini in boiling water and let soak for 10 minutes. Remove the mushrooms and check the liquid. If the liquid appears sandy soak the mushrooms for 3 additional minutes; if not, add liquid to the mushroom stock.

■ Melt the butter in a wide pot and sauté onions and garlic for 1 minute. When onions are translucent, add sliced mushrooms, salt, pepper, and sherry, and cook uncovered until mushrooms are soft. Add the mushroom stock. Place all the herbs in the cheesecloth and tie well, add to the soup.

■ Bring to a boil and reduce to a simmer. Let cook uncovered for 30 minutes. Remove the cheesecloth and ladle soup into serving bowls. Serve with cheese crackers.

LIGHT DILL & ZUCCHINI SOUP
Serves 4

8 medium green zucchini
1 onion
4 garlic cloves, minced
8 cups vegetable stock
2 tablespoons olive oil
1 cup fresh dill, chopped
Salt and pepper
Fried noodles or toast points for garnish

■ Wash zucchini well and cut into half-inch pieces. Peel and dice the onion. Warm oil and sauté the onion and garlic in a big high pot for 2-3 minutes (until translucent). Add zucchini and vegetable stock and season with salt and pepper. Bring to a boil and reduce to a simmer. Cover and let cook for 25 minutes then remove lid and continue cooking for 15 minutes.

■ Remove from the heat. Puree with an emulsifying blender or in a food processor; add dill and check for flavor. The soup should be thick and rich in texture. If it is too thin continue cooking for 10 more minutes without a lid.

■ Pour into serving bowls and top with some fried noodles or two toast points.

1/3 cup olive oil
1 pound stew meat, cubed (1/2-inch)
2 quarts beef/chicken stock
Salt and pepper
1/3 cup barley
2 onions, thinly sliced
2 cloves garlic, minced
2 stalks celery, diced
1 leek, thinly sliced
1 carrot, cut in half lengthwise and thinly sliced
1 bay leaf
1 large sprig of fresh thyme
12 ounces pumpkin, peeled and cut into small dices
2 medium potatoes cut into small dices
1/2 cup fresh or frozen lima beans or fava beans
1/2 cup fresh or frozen green peas
2 small zucchinis, cut in half lengthwise and thinly sliced
2 ripe tomatoes, peeled and roughly chopped
2 pounds marrow bones
1 cup chopped fresh string beans
16-ounce can tomato puree
2 tablespoons chopped fresh parsley
6 toast points
Sea salt

Preheat oven to 400 degrees F.

■ Place the bones on a baking sheet and bake for about 25-30 minutes until dark brown. Season diced meat with salt and pepper. Heat the oil in a big pot and sauté the seasoned meat for 3 minutes, mixing occasionally, until meat is golden on all sides. Remove the meat and sauté the onion, garlic, celery and leeks for 2 minutes; add the meat, stock, barley, bay leaf, thyme and bones and season well with salt and pepper. Bring to a boil and remove the foam that emerges to the top. Lower flame and simmer covered for 1 1/2 hours.

■ Add the rest of the vegetables, tomato puree, and parsley. Cook for an additional 40 minutes.

■ Remove the bones and use a small knife to remove the bone marrow. Spread the bone marrow on the toast points and sprinkle with the sea salt. Ladle the soup into serving bowls and serve hot with a toast point.

CREATING A DISH IS LIKE TOURING THE
WORLD, TAKING DIFFERENT FLAVORS AND
TEXTURES FROM EACH CONTINENT TO CREATE
A SYMBOL OF PERFECTION.

SALADS

COLORFUL NICOISE SALAD WITH GRILLED FRESH TUNA

Serves 4-6

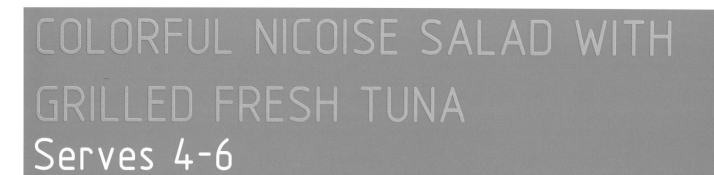

For the Dressing:

1/2 cup lemon juice
1 tablespoon chopped shallot
1 small garlic clove minced
1 teaspoon Dijon mustard
1 cup extra virgin olive oil
Salt and black pepper

For the Salad:

1 pound mixed salad greens
1 cup basil leaves (not packed)
1 red onion, thinly sliced
3 medium purple potatoes or new potatoes
1/2 pound cherry tomatoes (yellow, orange, red)
1/2 pound haricot vert (French green beans)
1 cup kidney beans, drained
4 ounces Nicoise olives, pitted
4 five-ounce tuna steaks
2 tablespoons olive oil for tuna
1 tablespoon fresh thyme leaves
Salt and pepper
4 hard-boiled eggs
1 cup capers, drained and dried
2 cups vegetable oil

reparation — Vinaigrette:

nisk the lemon juice, chopped shallot, garlic and mustard in a mixing wl. While whisking, add the oil slowly to create emulsification. ason with salt and pepper and check the flavors. If the vinaigrette is o tart add a little more oil; if too "oily" add more lemon juice and ustard.

reparation — Salad:

Cook the haricot vert in salted, boiling water for 2 minutes and move to ice water to stop the cooking process.

Cook the potatoes in salted water until soft but not falling apart neck with a fork). Drain, cool and cut into quarters.

Cut the cherry tomatoes in halves and the hard-boiled eggs into arters.

■ Warm the oil in a small high saucepan to 350 degrees F and carefully add the capers. If the capers are still wet splashing will occur. Transfer to a plate lined with paper towel to get rid of excess oil.

■ Bring a grilling pan or a griddle to high heat (a sauté pan or a non-stick pan can also be used). Brush the tuna steaks with the olive oil, season with salt and pepper and sprinkle with the thyme leaves. Place the steaks in a grilling pan and grill each side for one minute. Remove from the heat.

■ Mix the greens, tomatoes, beans, green beans, basil, potatoes and anchovy; toss with the vinaigrette and place the eggs and the tuna randomly on the salad. Drizzle with vinaigrette and serve.

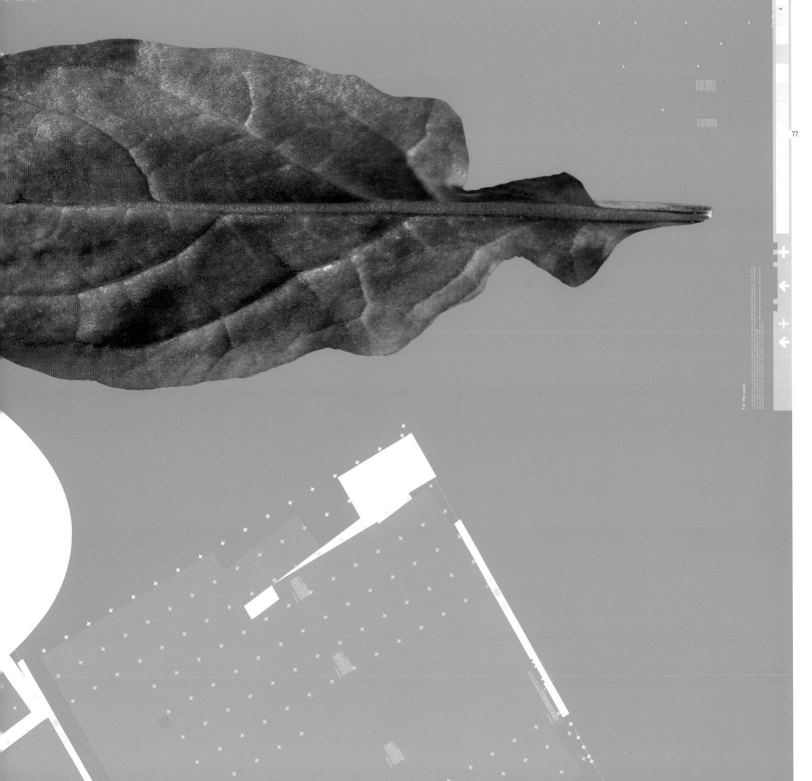

CITRUS AND AVOCADO SALAD WITH BABY ARUGULA AND HONEY-MUSTARD VINAIGRETTE

Serves 4

2 ripe avocados, sliced 1/2-inch thick
2 oranges, segmented, reserving 1 tablespoon juice
1 grapefruit, segmented
3 ounces baby arugula leaves
1 teaspoon finely grated orange rind
3 tablespoon extra virgin olive oil
1 tablespoon balsamic vinegar
1/2 teaspoon Dijon mustard
1 teaspoon honey
1 tablespoon chopped fresh mint

■ Place the avocados and citrus fruit in a serving bowl or platter and toss gently with baby arugula leaves. In a separate bowl, place the orange rind, juice, oil, vinegar, mustard and sugar. Season with salt and pepper and whisk together.

■ Pour over the salad and cover all the leaves and the fruit.

■ Sprinkle with the chopped mint and serve immediately.

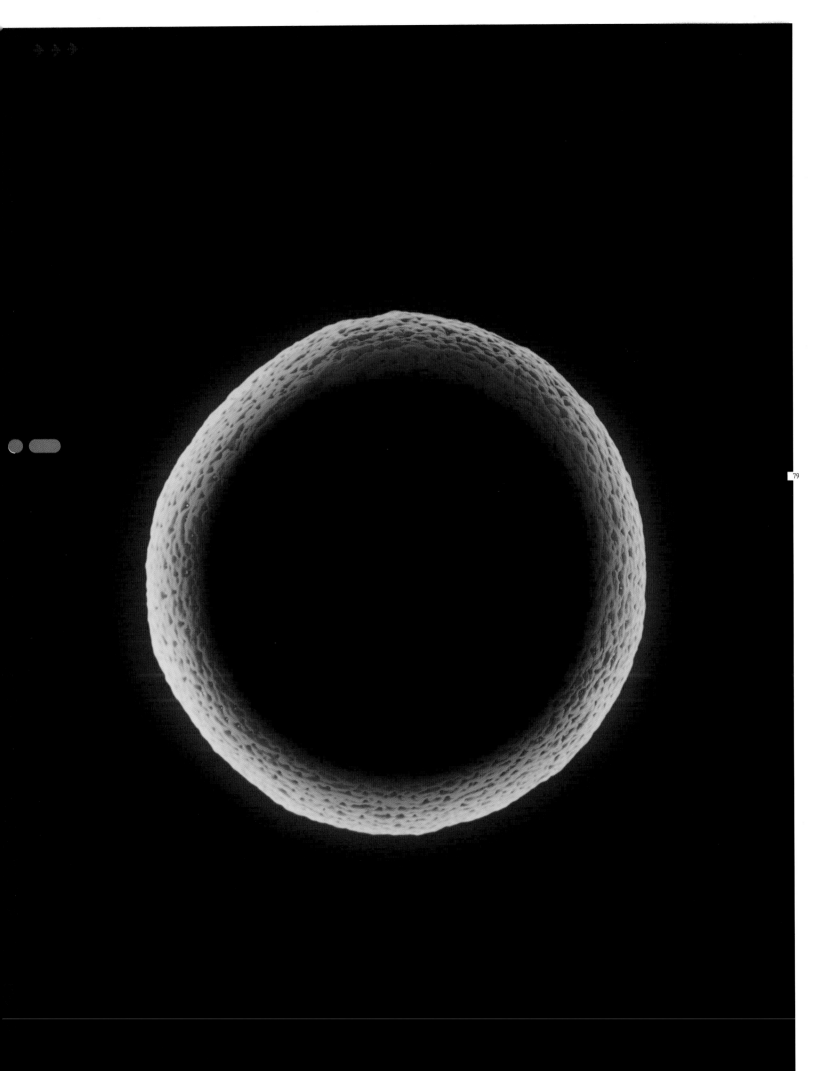

GREEK SALAD WITH SAUTÉED FETA CHEESE AND CRISPY GRAPE LEAVES

Serves 4

1 English cucumber, peeled
2 green peppers
4 vine-ripened tomatoes cut into wedges
1 red onion, finely sliced
16 Kalamata olives
12 ounces high quality firm Greek feta cheese diced 1/2-inch thick
2 eggs, beaten
1/2 cup wondra flour
1/3 cup olive oil
24 fresh flat-leaf parsley leaves
12 whole fresh mint leaves
1/2 cup good quality extra virgin olive oil
2 tablespoons lemon juice
1 clove garlic, crushed
4 grape leaves, washed well and completely dried
Vegetable oil for deep-frying

■ Cut the cucumber in half lengthwise and discard the seeds. Cut into 1/8-inch slices. Cut each pepper in half lengthwise, remove the membrane and seeds and cut the flesh into 1/8-inch wide strips.

■ Heat the vegetable oil to 375 degrees F. When hot enough deep-fry the grape leaves, two at a time, until translucent and crispy, about 45 seconds. Remove the leaves to a plate lined with paper towel.

■ Season the wondra flour with salt and pepper. Dip the feta cheese dices in the egg, get rid of excess egg and dredge them in the flour, shaking off extra flour. Heat the olive oil in a wide sauté pan until almost smoking and add the cheese. Sauté the dices for one minute until golden. Remove from the pan.

■ Gently mix the cucumber, green pepper, tomatoes, onion, olives, parsley and mint leaves in a large salad bowl. Add the cheese and toss lightly.

■ Whisk the oil, lemon juice and garlic in a small mixing bowl and season with salt and pepper. Pour over the salad and transfer into serving plates. Garnish with the crispy grape leaves and serve.

HUMMUS — MEDITERRANEAN CHICK-PEA PASTE

Serves 4-6

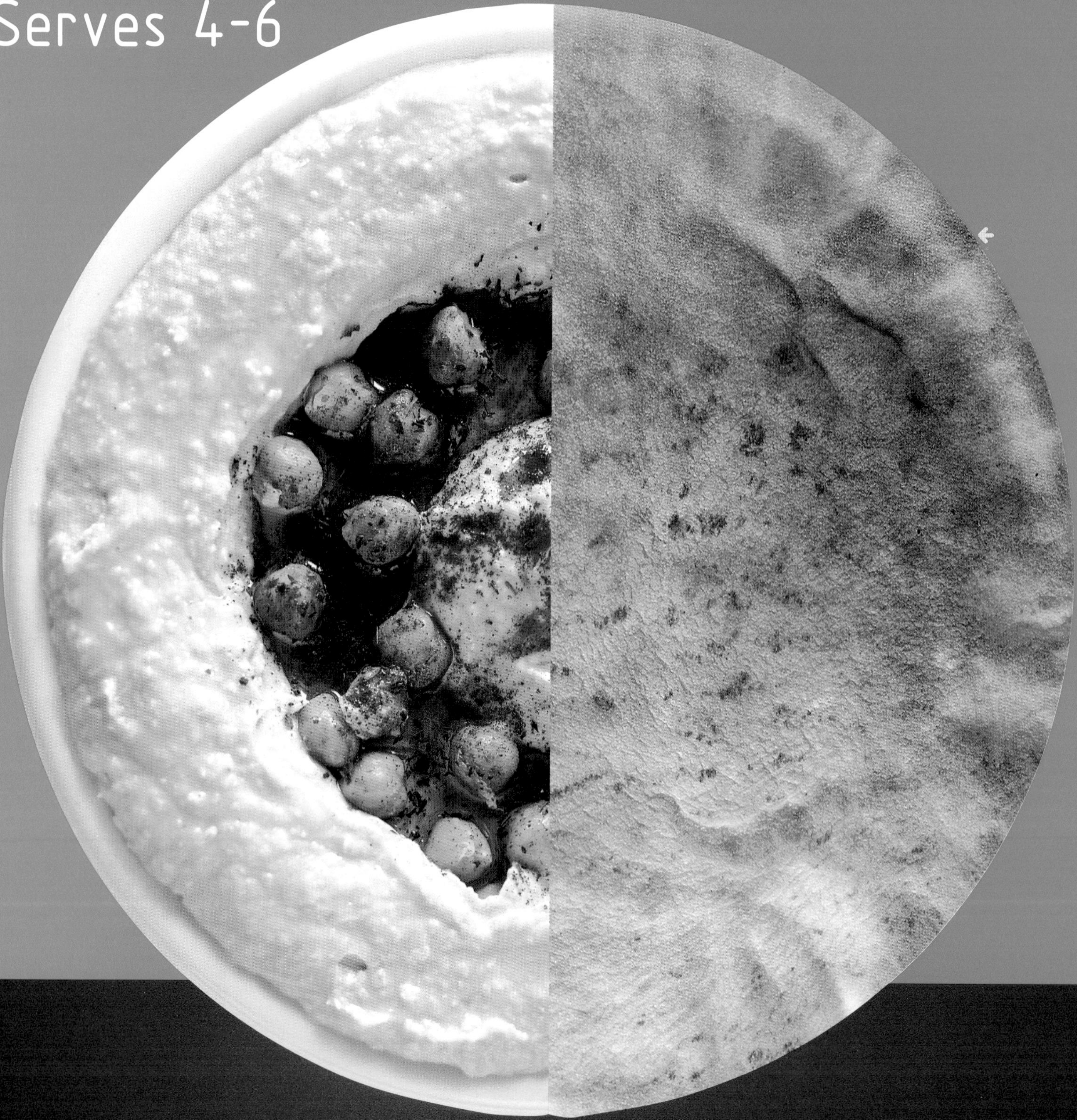

■ Place the chickpeas in a bowl, add 1 quart water, and soak overnight. Drain and place in a large saucepan with 2 quarts water (or enough to cover the chickpeas by 2 inches), bay leaf, onion and a carrot. Bring to boil, then reduce to a simmer for about 45 minutes, or until the chickpeas are very tender. Skim surface.

■ Discard the onion, carrot and bay leaf. Drain well reserving the cooking liquid and leave until cool enough to handle. Pick through for any loose skins and discard.

■ Blend the chickpeas, tahini, garlic, cumin, lemon juice, olive oil, cayenne pepper and 1/4 teaspoon salt in a food processor until thick and smooth. With the motor running, gradually add enough of the reserved cooking liquid, about 3/4 cup, to form a smooth creamy purée. Season with salt and lemon juice. Spread onto flat bowls or plates, drizzle with extra virgin olive oil, sprinkle with paprika and scatter parsley over the top. Serve with warm pita bread.

1 carrot, quartered
1 cup dried chickpeas
1 bay leaf
1 onion, quartered
2 tablespoons tahini
4 cloves garlic, crushed
2 teaspoons ground cumin
1/3 cup lemon juice
3 tablespoons olive oil
Large pinch of cayenne pepper
Extra virgin olive oil, to garnish
Paprika, to garnish
Chopped fresh flat-leaf parsley, to garnish

MIDDLE EASTERN CHOPPED SALAD
Serves 4-6

4 large tomatoes
2 cucumbers
1 red or green pepper
1 scallion
2 cloves garlic, minced
1 tablespoon minced fresh parsley
Salt and freshly ground black pepper
3 tablespoons olive oil
3 tablespoons lemon juice
1 teaspoon Za'atar (optional)

Wash tomatoes and dice small. Peel cucumbers and dice. Dice pepper. Finely chop scallions. Place all vegetables in a salad bowl, add remaining ingredients and mix well. Refrigerate until ready to serve. Before serving toss with Za'atar and serve with a crusty bread.

CARROT, PEARL BARLEY AND LIMA BEAN SALAD
Serves 4

1 pound carrots, peeled and diced small
1 cup pearl barley
3 cups vegetable stock
1 tablespoon vegetable oil
1 cup lima beans
2 tablespoons olive oil
1 clove garlic, chopped
1 teaspoon ground cumin
1/4 cup lime juice
2 scallions, green part only, finely sliced
3 tablespoons finely chopped cilantro
Salt and pepper

■ Sauté the barley in the vegetable oil for 30 seconds; add the vegetable stock and season with salt and pepper. Bring to a boil and reduce to a simmer. Let barley cook until tender (about 15 minutes).

■ When done, drain the excess liquids and let cool. Cook the lima beans in salted boiling water for 2 minutes, transfer to ice cold water to stop the cooking and drain.

■ Heat the olive oil in a wide sauté pan and add the garlic and ground cumin. Sauté for 10 seconds and add the diced carrots. Season well with salt and pepper and sauté for 3 additional minutes. Remove from the heat.

■ Combine the carrots (with the oil), barley and lima beans in a big mixing bowl. Toss with the lime juice and mix in the cilantro and scallions. Check for flavor and season accordingly. Serve at room temperature.

EGGPLANT SALAD WITH PESTO SAUCE AND ROASTED PINE NUTS

Serves 4-6

3 medium eggplants, diced (1/2-inch thick)
Vegetable oil for deep-frying
3 packed cups, fresh basil leaves, washed and dried
4 garlic cloves
2/3 cup extra virgin olive oil
1 tablespoon lemon juice
1 cup pine nuts, roasted

Heat oil to 375 degrees F.

■ Fry the eggplant, in batches, until golden brown and crispy. To avoid frying Preheat oven to 400 degrees F. Toss the eggplant dices with 1 cup olive oil and spread them on a sheet pan. Roast in the oven for 20 minutes. Remove from the oil to a baking sheet lined with paper towels. Let cool.

Preparation – Pesto:

■ Blend the basil and garlic for 15 seconds then slowly add the oil while blending, until a thick paste is achieved (all the oil may not be needed). Blend in the lemon juice and season well with salt and pepper.

■ Gently mix the eggplant with the pesto in a big mixing bowl. Transfer to a serving plate and toss with the pine nuts. Serve at room temperature.

POTATO AND SAUTÉED APPLE SALAD IN LIGHT CIDER VINAIGRETTE

Serves 4

■ Place unpeeled potatoes in a 4-quart pot. Cover with water, salt well and cook for approximately 30 minutes. Rinse in cold water. While potatoes are still warm, peel and dice.

■ Heat the olive oil, add garlic and sauté for 20 seconds. Add the apple dices, mixing for 2 minutes and remove from the pan; season with salt and pepper and let cool.

■ In the same pan, melt the butter and add the onion slices. Cook over high flame until onions are lightly golden and toss with the brown sugar. Reduce to a medium heat and keep cooking until the onions are soft and caramelized. Remove from the pan.

■ Mix the cider vinegar, apple cider and mayonnaise in a small mixing bowl; slowly add the oil while whisking. Season with salt and pepper.

■ Combine the potatoes with the vinaigrette in a big mixing bowl. Add the onions, chopped herbs and apples. Check the seasoning and correct accordingly.

■ Serve at room temperature as part of a salad plate or as a side dish.

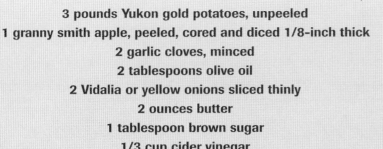

3 pounds Yukon gold potatoes, unpeeled
1 granny smith apple, peeled, cored and diced 1/8-inch thick
2 garlic cloves, minced
2 tablespoons olive oil
2 Vidalia or yellow onions sliced thinly
2 ounces butter
1 tablespoon brown sugar
1/3 cup cider vinegar

1 tablespoon mayonnaise
2 tablespoons apple cider
1 cup grape seed oil
Salt and pepper
1/4 cup chopped basil leaves
1/4 cup chopped mint leaves
Salt and pepper

SUMMER TOMATO SALAD WITH ANCHOVY-FLAVORED CROUTONS AND BALSAMIC-PARMESAN VINAIGRETTE

Serves 6

1/2 cup extra virgin olive oil
2 cloves garlic, peeled and pounded
2 to 3 anchovy fillets, rinsed and patted dry
Salt and freshly ground black pepper
1/2 loaf Italian country bread or sour bread, crust removed and cut into 1/2-inch cubes
3 red heirloom tomatoes
2 yellow tomatoes
2 orange tomatoes
1/3 cup aged balsamic vinegar
1 cup extra virgin olive oil
1 teaspoon Worcestershire sauce
1/2 cup Parmesan grated cheese
1/2 cup basil leaves, washed and dried

Preheat oven to 350 degrees F.
■ Chop the anchovy fillets with the salt or mash them with a fork.

■ Heat the oil in a small saucepan; add the garlic and chopped anchovies. Cook for 20 seconds and remove from the heat. Discard the garlic.

■ Place the diced bread in a mixing bowl and drizzle the seasoned oil on top while tossing to make sure they are evenly flavored.

■ Spread on a baking sheet and bake, shaking the pan once or twice, until golden brown, 10 to 15 minutes. Whisk the Worcestershire sauce and the balsamic vinegar in a small bowl. While whisking, add the olive oil slowly to create emulsification (hand blender can be used as well). Add the Parmesan and season with salt and pepper. Taste and correct flavors as needed.

■ Remove the tips of the tomatoes and cut them in halves. Discard the seeds and dice 1/2-inch thick.

■ Toss the tomatoes with the vinaigrette in a large mixing bowl; add the croutons and toss briefly. Transfer to a serving plate and garnish with the fresh basil leaves. Serve immediately.

COCONUT, CABBAGE AND CARROT COLESLAW
Serves 4-6

1 small red or green cabbage
1/4 cup lemon juice
2 large carrots, grated
1 fresh coconut, peeled and grated or 11/2 cups
unsweetened coconut flakes
1 shallot, minced
1/2 cup mayonnaise
2 tablespoons lemon juice
1 teaspoon salt
2 tablespoons sugar
1/2 teaspoon curry powder
1/2 cup toasted coconut flakes (optional)
1/4 cup chopped dill for garnish

■ Shred or grate cabbage as desired. Mix the cabbage with the lemon juice and let stand in the refrigerator for a couple of hours or overnight. Drain the cabbage of excess liquids.

■ Combine the carrots, cabbage and coconut in a large bowl. In a separate small bowl, combine the mayonnaise, lemon juice, sugar and curry and mix well. Add dressing to vegetables and toss until coated. Cover and refrigerate until ready to serve.

■ Before serving mix the salad again and check for flavor; season accordingly. Toss with the chopped dill and top with the toasted coconut flakes.

GRILLED ENDIVE & ARUGULA SALAD WITH HONEY-TOASTED WALNUTS IN HORSERADISH VINAIGRETTE

Serves 4-6

4 endives, cut to quarters, lengthwise (and/or radicchio)
3 bunches (handfuls) arugula, washed and dried
1/2 cup very good extra virgin olive oil
Salt and black pepper
1/4 cup brown sugar
Shredded carrots for garnish

For Honey-toasted Walnuts:
2 cups walnuts
2/3 cup honey
1 tablespoon onion powder
1 teaspoon garlic powder
2 pinches salt
2 pinches cayenne pepper

For the Horseradish Vinaigrette:
(makes 1 1/2 cups of dressing)
1 shallot, chopped
2 tablespoons white horseradish
1 tablespoon sour cream (or mayo)
1-2 tablespoons applesauce
Salt and black pepper
1/3 cup cider vinegar
1 cup olive oil

Preparation – Nuts:

Preheat oven to 300 degrees F.

■ Mix all ingredients together in a mixing bowl, transfer to a baking sheet and toast for 15 minutes (rotating the baking sheet) or until walnuts are almost dark brown. Let cool completely before using.

■ Heat a grilling pan or griddle. Rub the endive quarters with olive oil and season with salt and pepper. Sprinkle with brown sugar and grill all sides until the endives are tender (endives can be "marked" by the grill and placed in a preheated oven for 5 minutes to finish the cooking).

Preparation – Vinaigrette:

■ Mix shallots, horseradish, salt, pepper and sour cream. Add the vinegar and mix well. Drizzle the oil slowly while mixing to a smooth thick texture. (Can be done with emulsifier blender or in a food processor.)

■ Toss the arugula and honey roasted nuts with 1/2 cup of the vinaigrette in a mixing bowl (add more if needed). In another mixing bowl toss the grilled endive with 1/4 cup of vinaigrette.

■ Pile the arugula nicely on a plate, lean endives on the arugula around the plate. Sprinkle with shredded carrots.

GREEN AND RED LEAVES SALAD WITH DRIED CRANBERRIES, PINEAPPLE-MANGO AND VODKA VINAIGRETTE

Serves 4-6

2 heads frisee lettuce
2 cups red oak leaves or beet greens
1/2 cup dried cranberries
3 ounces Roquefort cheese or Gorgonzola, crumbled (optional)

For the Vinaigrette:
1 cup diced ripe mango
1/2 cup crushed pineapple
1/3 cup vodka (can be flavored)
3 tablespoons sour cream
2 tablespoons white wine vinegar
1/2 -2/3 cup grape seed oil
1 teaspoon honey
Salt and pepper

■   Wash the lettuce and red leaves in cold water and dry well in a lettuce spinner. Place in a big bowl and toss with the cranberries and cheese.

Preparation — Vinaigrette:
■ Place the mango and crushed pineapple in a food processor and puree for 30 seconds. Add the sour cream, vodka and vinegar and puree well. While working, drizzle the oil to create emulsification. Add the honey and season well with salt and pepper.

■ Drizzle some of the vinaigrette over the salad and toss. Check for flavor and seasoning.

TOMATO SALAD WITH WARM GOAT CHEESE, SHAVED RED ONIONS IN WARM BALSAMIC VINAIGRETTE

Serves 4

1 red beefsteak tomato
2 cherry tomatoes
2 yellow tomatoes
1 orange tomato
8-ounce log of fresh goat cheese (like chevre) cut into 8 one-ounce round pieces
8 thin slices of baguette (French bread)
1/3 cup basil leaves, washed and dried

2 tablespoons olive oil
Sea salt
1 shallot, finely diced
1/2 cup good balsamic vinegar
1 teaspoon Dijon mustard
1 cup extra virgin olive oil
Salt and pepper

Preheat oven to 350 degrees F.

■ Brush the baguette slices with the olive oil and place one piece of goat cheese on top. Transfer to a baking sheet and place in the oven for 4 minutes.

■ Wash the tomatoes and slice thinly. Julienne basil. Arrange the tomatoes on serving plates, alternating the colors, and sprinkle with the sea salt. Top with two goat cheese toasts and sprinkle with the basil strips.

■ Heat 1 tablespoon of the extra virgin olive oil in a saucepot and sauté the shallots for 2 minutes. Add the balsamic vinegar and the mustard and whisk vigorously for 1 minute. Turn off the heat and add the rest of the oil slowly while whisking. Season with salt and pepper and drizzle over the tomato salad. Serve immediately.

GRILLED CHICKEN BREAST AND CURRIED PEACH SALAD
Serves 4

2 chicken breasts
2 tablespoons olive oil
1 tablespoon fresh rosemary leaves
Salt and pepper
6 hard peaches
1/4 cup lime juice
1 teaspoon curry powder
1 garlic clove, minced
2 tablespoons grape seed oil
1/3 cup thinly sliced scallions
1 head boston lettuce, leaves washed, dried and torn

Preheat oven to 370 degrees F.

■ Rub the chicken breasts in olive oil, season well with salt and pepper and sprinkle with the rosemary leaves. Heat a grill pan or a griddle and grill the breasts for 3 minutes on each side. Remove from the pan and place in the oven for 7 minutes.

■ Bring a pot with water to a boil. Cook the peaches for 2 minutes and transfer to cold water. Peel the peaches, remove the pit and slice (1/4-inch thick). Heat the oil in a small saucepan, add the garlic and the curry and sauté for 30 seconds. Remove from the heat. Add the peaches and the lime juice and let stand for 5 minutes.

■ Slice each breast on the bias into 1/8-inch thick slices and gently mix with the peaches.

■ Arrange the lettuce leaves on serving plates; top with the chicken and curried peaches, sprinkle with the scallions and serve.

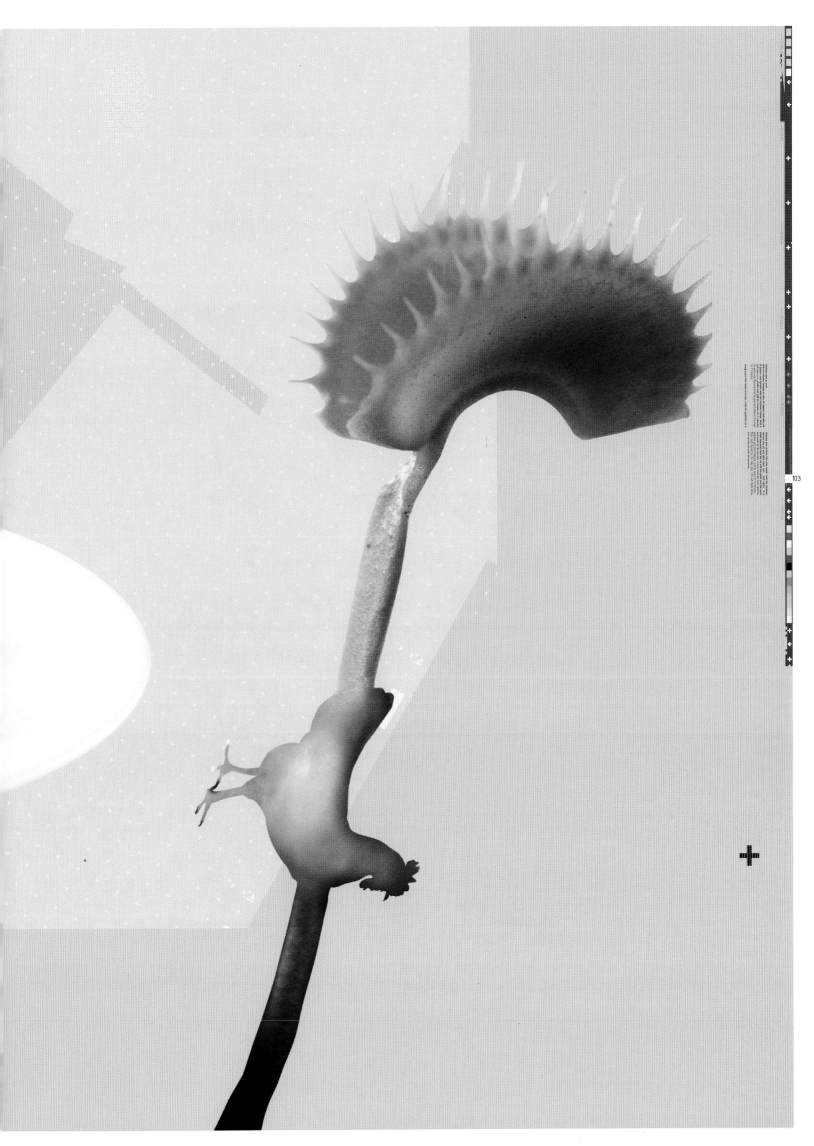

COOKING IS A WAY TO EXPRESS YOURSELF. A RECIPE IS JUST THE TOOL YOU USE TO DO IT WELL.

PASTA

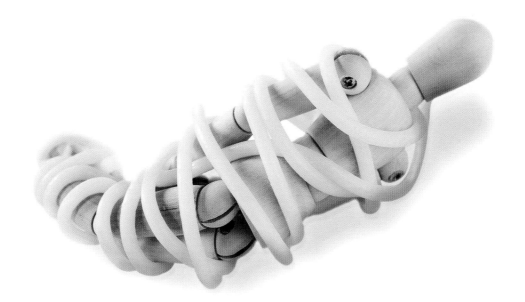

PENNE WITH LEMON AND POPPY SEED SAUCE
Serves 4

1 pound penne
2 tablespoons unsalted butter at room temperature
2 shallots, finely diced
1 cup light cream
1/2 cup poppy seeds
1/3 cup freshly squeezed lemon juice
1 tablespoon lemon zest
3 tablespoons fresh Italian parsley, chopped
1/4 cup freshly grated or shaved Parmesan cheese

■ Cook the penne in a large pot of boiling water until al dente (about 8 minutes) and drain.

■ Grind the poppy seeds in a spice grinder for 10 seconds. Heat the butter in a skillet large enough to hold the cooked pasta, and sauté the shallots and poppy seeds for 1 minute. Add the cream and lemon zest and bring to a boil, reduce to a simmer and let cook for 10 minutes over a low heat.

■ When sauce thickens, add lemon juice and season with salt and pepper. Add the cooked pasta to the skillet, away from the heat and toss to blend.

■ Let stand covered for about 2 minutes allowing the pasta to absorb the sauce. Serve with a sprinkle of fresh parsley and shaved cheese.

GEMELLI WITH ARTICHOKE HEARTS, KIDNEY BEANS AND TARRAGON

Serves 4

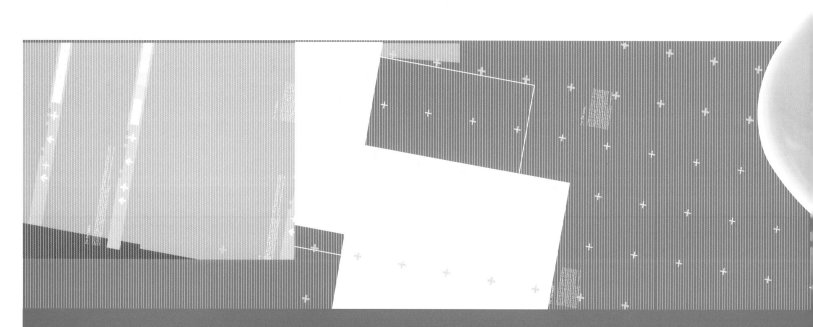

1 package gemelli pasta
8 ounces artichoke hearts, frozen and thawed
2 cups cooked kidney beans, drained
2 garlic cloves, sliced
4 stems fresh tarragon + 1/4 cup fresh tarragon leaves
1 teaspoon fennel seeds
1 cup olive oil
6 ounces smoked turkey breast, diced
Salt and pepper

■ Heat the oil with the tarragon stems and the fennel seeds in a small pot for 3 minutes. Turn off the heat and let stand so that the oil will be infused with the tarragon flavor until ready to be used. For better results do this a day or two in advance.

■ In a pot with boiling salted water, cook the artichoke hearts for 2 minutes; remove from the water to a bowl with ice-cold water to stop the cooking. Cook the pasta in the same pot until al dente (about 8-10 minutes) and drain.

■ Strain the infused oil and heat 1/3 of a cup in a wide sauté pan. Add the garlic and sauté for 30 seconds then add the artichoke hearts and the diced turkey breast and sauté for 2 more minutes. Add the beans and season well with salt and pepper. Add the pasta and cook while stirring occasionally for 1-2 minutes; toss with the tarragon leaves.

■ Apportion the pasta to serving plates and drizzle with a little of the remaining oil.

SPAGHETTI IN GARLIC AND OLIVE OIL

Serves 4

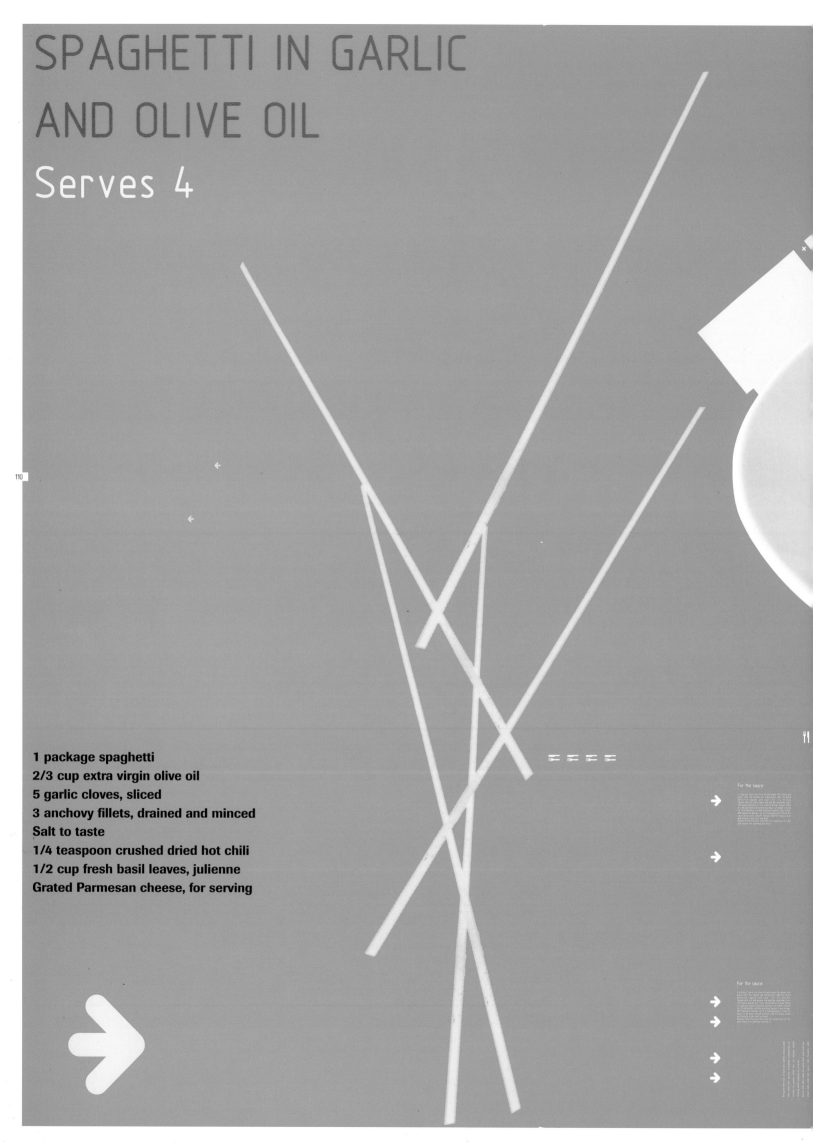

1 package spaghetti
2/3 cup extra virgin olive oil
5 garlic cloves, sliced
3 anchovy fillets, drained and minced
Salt to taste
1/4 teaspoon crushed dried hot chili
1/2 cup fresh basil leaves, julienne
Grated Parmesan cheese, for serving

■ Cook the pasta in hot boiling salted water in a large pot until al dente (about 8-10 minutes). Drain well.

■ Heat the oil in a heavy-bottomed sauté pan or skillet. Add the garlic and anchovies over low heat and cook until the garlic just begins to take on a hint of color. Do not brown the garlic since it will turn bitter. Remove from heat.

■ Add the cooked pasta and the basil to the seasoned oil. Toss well and season to taste with salt and the chili flakes.

■ Apportion to individual pasta dishes. Sprinkle each portion with parsley. Top with the cheese, and serve immediately.

SPAGHETTI WITH ROASTED CHERRY TOMATOES, FENNEL AND SAFFRON SAUCE

Serves 4

1 package Spaghetti

2 pints cherry tomatoes (can be different colors)

1/2 cup extra virgin olive oil

2 stems fresh thyme

1 stem fresh rosemary

1 fennel bulb, diced (keep the fennel leaves for garnish)

2 garlic cloves, minced

3 tablespoons olive oil or butter

2 cups dry white wine

1/3 teaspoon high quality saffron threads

Salt and pepper

1/3 cup grated Parmesan cheese (optional)

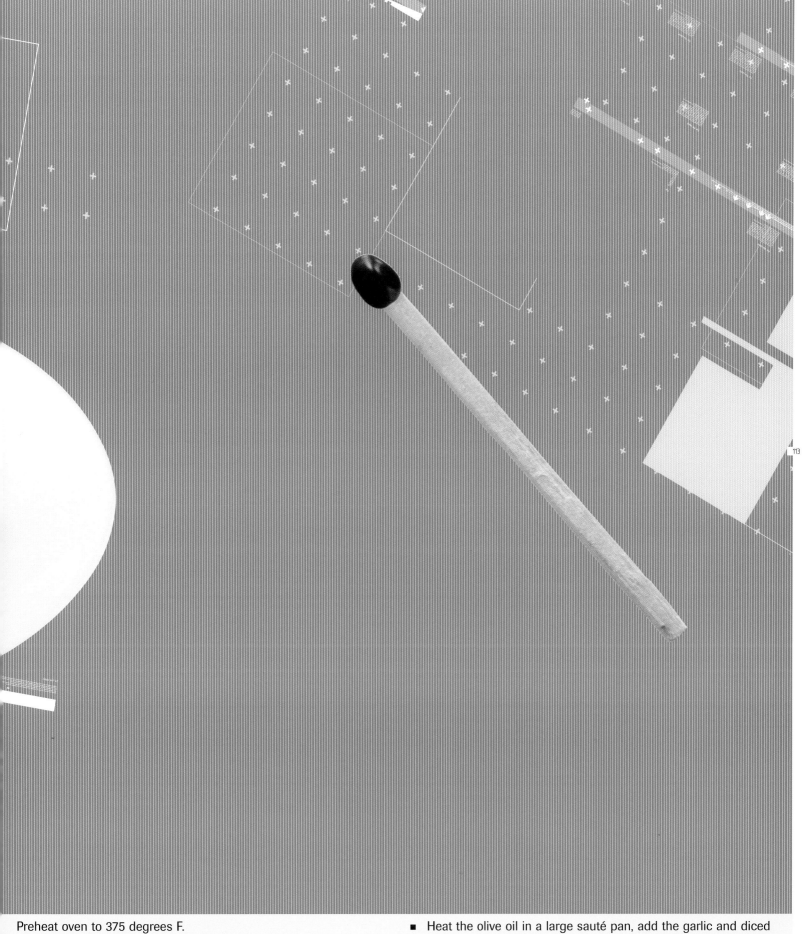

Preheat oven to 375 degrees F.

■ Toss the cherry tomatoes in a mixing bowl with the extra virgin olive oil, thyme and rosemary stems and season well with salt and pepper. Spread the tomatoes on a baking sheet and roast in the oven for 10-15 minutes, mixing once, until the tomatoes are lightly brown. Remove from the oven and let cool.

■ Cook the pasta in a pot with boiling salted water until al dente (about 8-10 minutes) and drain.

■ Heat the olive oil in a large sauté pan, add the garlic and diced fennel and cook for 4 minutes. Add the saffron and wine and bring to a boil, allowing the liquid to reduce by half. Season well with salt and pepper. Add the pasta and the roasted tomatoes and cook until thoroughly warm (about 2 minutes).

■Apportion pasta to serving plates, sprinkle the cheese, garnish with the fennel leaves and serve warm.

GOAT CHEESE RAVIOLI WITH ZUCCHINI AND TOMATO SAUCE
Serves 4

2 1/2 cups unbleached all purpose flour
1 egg + 2 extra large egg yolks
2 tablespoons extra virgin olive oil
1/4 cup cold water
1/2 teaspoon salt
8 ounces soft goat cheese
2 ounces Pecorino Romano cheese, grated
1 garlic clove, minced
1 egg + 1 egg, beaten, for sealing ravioli
2 small zucchini, sliced 1/4-inch thick

1 small onion, cut into thin wedges
1 (14 1/2 ounce) can diced tomatoes
2 tablespoons olive oil
1/2 teaspoon thyme leaves
1 teaspoon chopped fresh tarragon
1 tablespoon chopped fresh basil
2 tablespoons black olives, pitted and sliced
2 tablespoons shredded fresh Parmesan cheese
Salt and pepper

■ Place the flour on a working surface and create a well in the center. Beat the yolks and the egg; add in the water, salt and oil and place in the center. Use a fork to begin incorporating the flour into the egg mixture, adding small amounts at a time. When the dough is thick enough start working with your hands until you get a smooth elastic finish. Clean the working area, lightly flour it, then roll the dough (use a pasta machine if one is available) into a thin sheet. Combine the cheeses, garlic and egg in a mixing bowl.

■ Roll the pasta sheet over a ravioli pan or cut out ravioli shapes using a cutter if ravioli pan is not available. Place a teaspoon of the filling in the center of half of the ravioli; brush the beaten egg around the edges and top with the empty cut out ravioli tightening the ravioli well with your thumb and index finger.

■   Bring a pot with salted water to a boil and cook ravioli for 2 minutes. Drain, cover and keep warm.

■ Heat the oil in a wide sauté pan over medium-high heat. Add zucchini and onion; cook and stir 3 to 4 minutes or until vegetables are crisp and tender.

■ Add tomatoes, herbs and olives and cook and stir for 5 minutes. Add cooked ravioli and stir gently.

■ Apportion raviolis to serving plates, sprinkle with the Parmesan cheese and serve.

ANGEL HAIR PASTA WITH PORCINI CRUSTED CHICKEN, SCALLIONS AND SHIITAKE MUSHROOMS

Serves 4

1 package angel hair pasta

4 boneless, chicken cutlets cut into bite-sized strips

4 tablespoons vegetable oil

1 cup dried porcini mushrooms

2/3 cup flour

2 eggs, beaten

1 onion, cut into thin wedges

2 scallions, green part only, cut into half-inch strips

1 cup chicken stock

8 ounces fresh shiitake mushrooms, stem removed (and kept), sliced

Salt and pepper

■ Cook the pasta in a pot of boiling salted water until al dente (about 8-10 minutes), drain.

■ In a spice grinder or a blender grind the dried porcini to a powder (if some chunks are left strain the powder). Place the flour, eggs and the porcini powder in three different plates one next to the other in that order. Season the chicken pieces with salt and pepper and dredge them in the flour getting rid of the excess flour by shaking them. Dip them in the beaten egg and dredge
them in the porcini powder to coat well.

■ Heat the oil in a wide sauté pan and stir fry the chicken strips for 3 minutes. Remove the chicken and add the onion wedges. Sauté for 2 minutes adding a little more oil if needed. Add the mushrooms and the chicken stock, scraping the bottom of the pan with a wooden spoon, and bring to a boil.

■ Reduce to medium heat and season well with salt and pepper. Let simmer until liquid is reduced by half.

■ Add the pasta and let cook for 2 minutes. Toss with the chicken strips and the scallion and remove from the heat. Apportion to serving plates and serve hot.

PENNE WITH CREAM OF ROASTED RED PEPPERS AND GORGONZOLA CHEESE

Serves 4

1 package penne pasta

5 red peppers

3 tablespoons olive oil

2 shallots

2 cloves garlic

1/3 cup sherry wine vinegar

1 cup olive oil

1/3 cup heavy cream

Salt and pepper

8 ounces good Gorgonzola cheese, crumbled

Basil for garnish

Preheat oven to 400 degrees F.

■ Brush the peppers with the olive oil and place on a baking sheet. Roast the peppers in the oven for about 30 minutes turning them often until all sides are slightly burnt. Remove from the oven to a big bowl and wrap well with saran wrap. Let the peppers "sweat" and cool for about 10 minutes and,

using your hands, peel them (the skin should come off easily) and discard the tips and the seeds. Place the roasted peppers in a blender along with the garlic, shallots vinegar and oil and puree to a smooth texture. Season well with salt and pepper.

■ Cook the pasta in a pot of boiling salted water until al dente (about 8-10 minutes), drain.

■　Transfer the red pepper sauce to a wide pan and heat over a medium flame. Add in the cream and mix until well combined. Taste and correct seasoning accordingly. Add the pasta and toss so that the it will be well coated in the sauce. Remove from the heat and mix in the Gorgonzola cheese.

■　Apportion   to serving plates, garnish with the basil leaves and serve.

VEGETABLE MACARONI IN PESTO SAUCE WITH SUN-DRIED TOMATOES AND HARD-BOILED EGGS

Serves 4

3 eggs

1 package macaroni pasta

1 tablespoon olive oil or vegetable oil

2 leeks, white part only, cleaned

2 carrots, peeled

1 zucchini

1/2 cup drained marinated sun-dried tomatoes (from 8-ounce jar), chopped

1/4 cup black olives, pitted

3 packed cups, fresh basil leaves, washed and dried

4 garlic cloves

2/3 cup extra virgin olive oil

1/2 cup pine nuts

Salt and pepper

2 tablespoons grated fresh Parmesan cheese

FETTUCCINE WITH LEEKS AND VERMOUTH CREAM SAUCE

Serves 4

1 pound good quality fettuccine
5 leeks, white part only
1-2 ounces butter
2/3 cup dry vermouth
1 tablespoon grainy mustard
Salt and pepper
3 garlic cloves, minced
2 cups heavy cream
1/4 cup thinly sliced basil leaves
Grated Parmesan cheese for serving

■ Bring a big pot (or a pasta pot) with water to a boil and salt the water well. Cook the pasta for 10 minutes or until al dente. Drain the pasta and set aside one cup of the cooking water.

■ Melt the butter in a big sauté pan, add the leeks and garlic and stir. Let cook over a medium heat for about 5 minutes until leeks start to soften and turn golden. Add the vermouth and reduce to low-medium heat, cook for 2 minutes, then add the cream and mustard. Season with salt and pepper and cook for 5-10 minutes or until the cream thickens. If the sauce is too thick add a little of the pasta cooking liquid.

■ Add the fettuccini and cook it in the sauce for 2 minutes. Add the sliced basil leaves and transfer to a serving platter. Sprinkle with grated Parmesan cheese.

SPAGHETTI PUTTANESCA
Serves 4

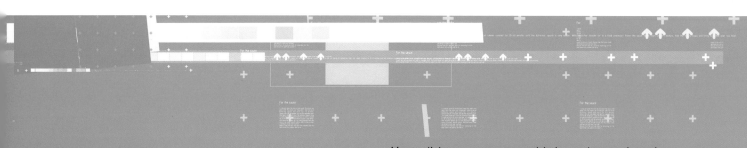

1 package spaghetti
1/3 cup olive oil
2 onions, finely chopped
3 cloves garlic, finely chopped
1/2 teaspoon chili flakes
6 large ripe tomatoes, diced
4 tablespoons capers, rinsed
8 anchovies in oil, drained, chopped
5 ounces Kalamata olives, pitted
3 tablespoons chopped fresh flat-leaf parsley

■ Heat oil in a saucepan, add the onion and cook over medium heat for 5 minutes. Add the garlic and chili flakes to the saucepan and cook for 30 seconds. Add the tomato, capers and anchovies. Simmer over low heat for 10-15 minutes, or until the sauce is thick and pulpy. Stir in the olives and the parsley.

■ While the sauce is cooking, cook the spaghetti in a large pot of boiling salted water until al dente. Drain and return to the pan.

■ Add the sauce to the pasta and stir through. Season with salt and freshly ground black pepper, to taste, and serve immediately.

FETTUCCINE ALFREDO WITH ASPARAGUS TIPS AND WALNUT OIL

Serves 4

8 ounces dried spinach fettuccine
4 tablespoons butter
1 garlic clove, minced
2/3 cup heavy cream
1 cup grated Parmesan cheese
1 bunch asparagus
1 tablespoon walnut oil
Cracked black pepper
2/3 cup roasted walnuts
Salt

■ Cut the top inch (tips) of the asparagus and cook briefly in boiling salted water (about 1 minute). Remove to a bowl with ice cold water to stop the cooking (keep the rest of the asparagus stems for a stock or to be used in another dish).

■ Cook the pasta in a pot of boiling salted water until al dente (about 8 minutes) and strain.

■ Heat the butter with the cream in a wide pot until melted. Stir in the Parmesan cheese and garlic and mix until sauce thickens, season with salt as needed. Add the pasta and asparagus tips and cook for 2 more minutes until pasta is well coated.

■ Apportion the pasta to serving plates, drizzle with the walnut oil and sprinkle with the roasted walnuts and black pepper

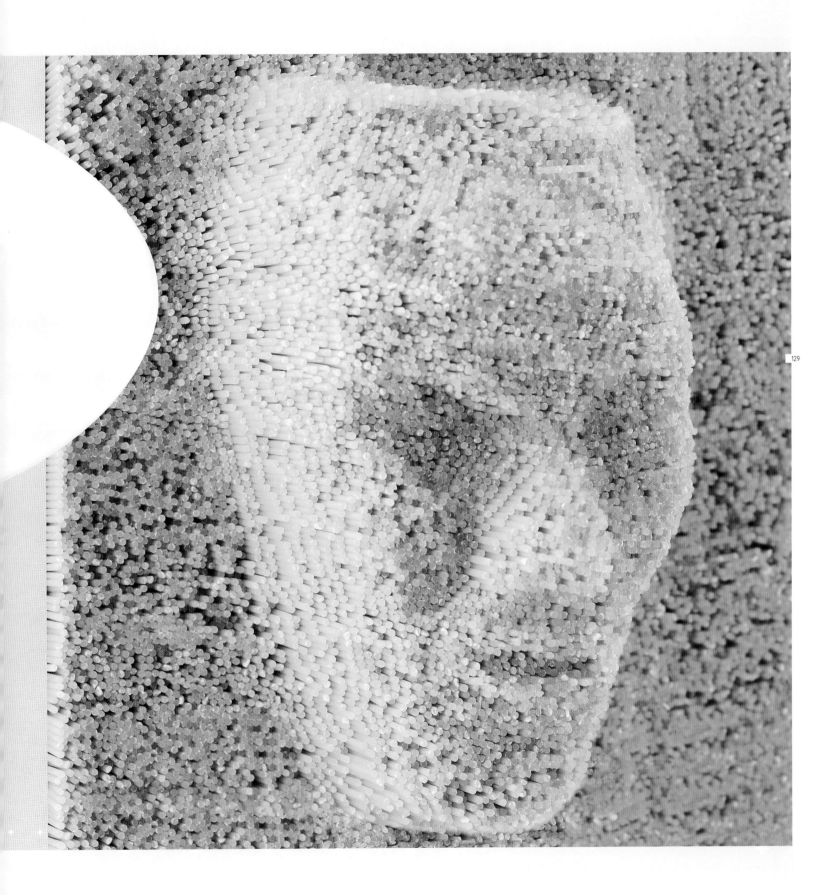

MANY THINGS CAN STIMULATE THE PASSION
TO COOK: GOING TO THE MARKET, EATING
OUT OR A DESIRE TO USE A BEAUTIFUL
SERVING PLATE. BE INSPIRED.

VEGETARIAN

AVOCADO AND SUN-DRIED TOMATO EGG ROLLS
Serves 6

6 egg roll skins
3 avocadoes, ripe but not too soft
1 8-ounce jar sun-dried tomatoes in oil (or sun-dried tomatoes,
soaked in hot water for 3 minutes until soft)
1 tablespoon lime juice
2 garlic cloves, minced
1 shallot, finely chopped
1/4 cup chopped scallions
1/4 teaspoon ground cumin
Salt and pepper
Oil for deep-frying (canola oil, peanut oil)
Mesculin greens for garnish

For the Dipping Sauce:

1/2 cup soy sauce
2 teaspoons sugar
2 tablespoons rice vinegar
2 tablespoons sliced scallions
1 tablespoon Miso paste
1 tablespoon minced ginger

Heat the oil to 350 degrees F.

■ Cut the avocadoes in half, discard the pit and spoon the avocadoes to a cutting board. Dice avocadoes (small) and drizzle with the lime juice.

■ Mix in the chopped shallots, garlic and cumin and season well with salt and pepper. Check for flavor and correct seasoning if needed.

■ On a working surface, spread the egg roll skins working with one at a time to prevent them from drying, and spread 2-3 tablespoons of the avocado salad (allowing a half-inch space from the edge). Drain the sun-dried tomatoes and spread about 4-5 on the avocado.

■ Brush the edges of the egg roll skin with water and quickly fold about an inch from the side inwards, towards the filling. Use your thumbs to roll the side that is close to you toward the far end. Roll gently to prevent stuffing from spilling out. Make sure the far end sticks to keep the rolls intact when frying.

■ Fry the rolls for about 2 minutes or until golden and crispy (if not completely fried after two minutes oil temperature was too low).

For the Dipping Sauce:

■ Heat soy sauce, sugar and ginger in a saucepan until sugar dissolves. Add rice vinegar, Miso and scallions.

■ Cut the roll on the bias. Season the greens with a little olive oil and salt and pile a small amount in the middle of each serving plate. Lean the cut roll against the greens, pour dipping sauce into small ramekins and place on the plate. Serve immediately.

STIR-FRIED RICE NOODLES WITH VEGETABLES
Serves 4

6 medium dried black mushrooms
1 medium carrot
4 ounces fresh peas
3 large stalks bok choy
3 green onions (with tops)
1 cup sliced canned bamboo shoots
1 tablespoon cornstarch
1 tablespoon water
8 ounces rice stick noodles
2 quarts water
2 tablespoons vegetable oil
2 teaspoons soy sauce
3 tablespoons vegetable oil
1/2 cup vegetable stock

■ Soak mushrooms in hot water for 20 minutes or until soft; drain. Rinse in warm water; drain. Squeeze out excess moisture. Remove and discard stems; cut caps into thin strips.

■ Cut carrot into 2-inch pieces, then slice lengthwise (1/8-inch). Bring a medium pot with water to a boil and salt the water well. Cook the carrots in the boiling water for 1-2 minutes and drain, keeping the water. Immediately transfer to a bowl with ice-cold water. Place peas in boiling water. Cover and cook 1 minute and transfer to a bowl with ice-cold water.

■ Remove leaves from bok choy stems and cut leaves into 2-inch pieces; cut stems diagonally into 1/2-inch slices (do not combine leaves and stems). Cut green onions diagonally into 1/2-inch pieces, and bamboo shoots lengthwise into thin strips. Mix cornstarch and 1 tablespoon water.

■ Pull noodles apart. Heat 2 quarts water to boiling point and stir in noodles. Cook uncovered 1 minute and drain. Rinse in cold water and drain again.

■ Heat wok until very hot. Add 3 tablespoons vegetable oil and tilt wok to coat side. Add mushrooms, bok choy stems and bamboo shoots; stir-fry 1 minute. Add stock and bring to a boil. Stir in cornstarch mixture; cook and stir until thickened. Stir in carrot, peas, bok choy leaves and green onions; heat to boiling. Pour vegetable mixture over noodles and serve hot.

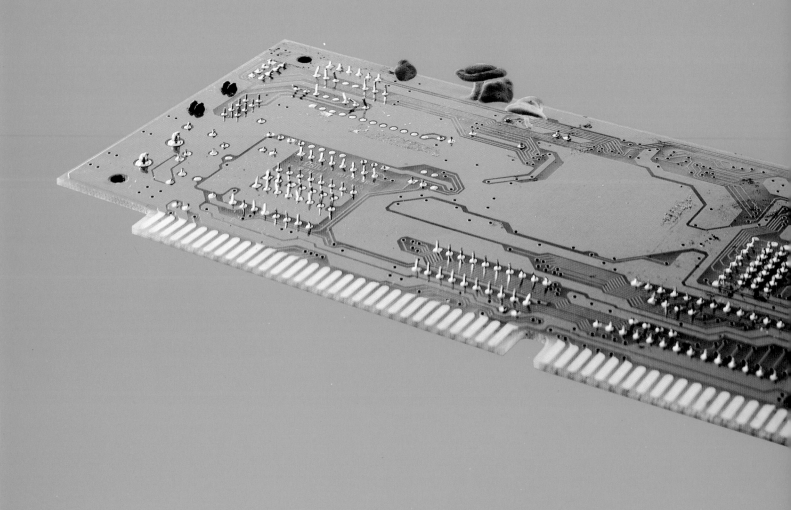

CELERIAC AND GREEN APPLE GRATIN
Serves 4

3 medium celeriac heads (celery root)
2 granny smith apples
2 cups heavy cream
2 shallots, chopped
3 garlic cloves, chopped
4 ounces + 1 tablespoon butter
1+1 teaspoon chopped fresh rosemary
1+1 teaspoon chopped fresh sage leaves
Salt and pepper
2 cups bread crumbs (preferably
homemade from sweet bread like challa or
brioche)
Endive, radicchio and romaine lettuce
leaves for garnish
2 tablespoons extra virgin olive oil
1 tablespoon balsamic vinegar

Heat oven to 375 degrees F.

■ Peel the celeriac heads and slice into thin, even slices, about 1/8-inch. Peel the apples, core them and slice, about 1/8 inch.

■ Sauté the garlic and shallots for two minutes. Remove from the heat and transfer to a mixing bowl. Add the cream, 1 teaspoon sage, 1 teaspoon rosemary and season well with salt and pepper.

■ Oil a square baking dish with olive oil. Arrange one layer of celeriac slices, overlapping. Top with a layer of the sliced apples, season with salt and pepper and drizzle with the cream. Repeat with the rest until half inch from the top of the dish. Cover with foil and bake for 45 minutes. While baking, melt the 4 ounces of butter and mix with the breadcrumbs and the remaining herbs; season with salt and pepper. Remove foil, spread the breadcrumb mixture evenly and bake for 20-30 minutes until golden and crisp. Remove from the oven, let cool for 15 minutes and then cut out serving portions, using a round cutter (optional).

■ Arrange endive, radicchio and romaine leaves on a serving plate alternating, for a nice presentation. Mix the olive oil and balsamic vinegar and drizzle over the greens. Place the gratin in the middle of the plate and serve.

EGGPLANT, PASTA & TAPANADE ROLLS
Serves 6

2 medium eggplants
1 cup olive oil
3 cups back olives, pitted
4 anchovy fillets
2 garlic cloves
1 teaspoon cider vinegar
1 box lasagna sheets, cooked
1 avocado
Salt and pepper

Preheat oven to 375 degrees F.

Preparation — Eggplants:

■ Slice the eggplants about 1/8-inch thick, lengthwise.

■ Drizzle half cup of the oil on a baking sheet and place the eggplant on it. Drizzle the remaining oil on the eggplants and place in the oven for 20-25 minutes (rotate in the oven, if needed). Let cool before assembling.

Preparation — Tapanade:

■ Place the olives, anchovies and vinegar in a food processor. Puree for 1 minute and add the garlic; puree until the garlic is chopped, and season with salt. Puree again for 30 seconds.

■ Cut the avocado in half, remove the pit, spoon each half onto a cutting board and slice thickly.

■ Line the working surface with saran wrap. Make two rows of overlapping eggplant slices, 5 per row, overlapping 1/4 of an inch, one on top of the other. Place one layer of the lasagna sheets on top and cover by spreading with a nice even layer of the tapanade. Line with the avocado slices.

■ Using both hands, roll the side close to you one rotation, while disengaging from the saran wrap. Continue to roll using the saran to help maintain the shape, but do not roll saran wrap into a roulade. The final roulade will be shaped into a log.

■ Refrigerate for 30 minutes. Before serving, slice the edges one-inch thick and serve with a salad.

LEEKS & GOAT CHEESE TART
Serves 4-6

For the dough:
2 cups all purpose flour
5 ounces cold unsalted flour, cut into small pieces
1/2 teaspoon salt
Pinch of sugar
1/4 cup ice-cold water

For the filling:
8 leeks, white part only, washed and cut into 1/8-inch slices (lengthwise)
1 ounce butter
1/3 cup dry Vermouth
Salt and pepper
1 cup heavy cream
2 whole eggs
1 egg yolk
1 tablespoon grainy mustard
6 ounces plain goat cheese, crumbled
Salt and pepper
Parchment paper
2 pounds beans, lentils or other dried legumes for blind baking

Preheat oven to 350 degrees F.

■ Mix together flour, salt and sugar by hand or in a food processor. Add the butter and work to a crumbly, sandy texture, about 30 seconds. Pour half of the water and mix for an additional 30 seconds. If dough appears dry add the rest of the water; if it starts to come together, transfer to a lightly floured surface. Quickly knead the dough with your hands to form a moist (but not too sticky dry dough). DO NOT overwork the dough, butter dots should still be visible. Shape the dough into a disk and refrigerate for at least 30 minutes.

■ Melt the butter in a big sauté pan. Add the leeks and cook 4-5 minutes over medium heat, stirring constantly. Add the Vermouth, season with salt and pepper and reduce to a low heat. Cook for about 15-20 minutes until leeks are soft. Let cool.

■ Grease a tart pan with butter or oil. On a lightly floured surface, roll the dough into a 10-inch diameter circle. Make sure the dough is evenly rolled. Layer the pan with the dough (bottom and walls) and press lightly to take out air pockets. Line the dough with parchment paper and pour the beans over spreading evenly. Bake for 15 minutes then remove the beans and the parchment and bake for an additional 10 minutes.

■ Whisk together the heavy cream, eggs, egg yolk, mustard, goat cheese and seasoning in a mixing bowl. Spread the leeks in the tart shell and slowly pour the cream/egg mixture, digging your fingers lightly into the leeks to allow the liquids to spread evenly. Bake for about 35-40 minutes until set. Serve warm or at room temperature.

MEDITERRANEAN GRILLED VEGETABLES OVER BROWN RICE
Serves 4-6

4 peppers (any color)
1 eggplant
4 zucchini
1 cauliflower
1/2 pound string beans
1/2 cup olive oil
Salt and pepper

For the Marinade:

1 cup extra virgin olive oil
1/3 cup Balsamic vinegar
1 cup grapeseed oil
1/3 cup red wine vinegar or apple cider vinegar
1/4 cup each of fresh herb leaves (oregano, thyme, basil, rosemary)
5 cloves garlic, thinly sliced
Salt and pepper
6 cups of cooked brown or wild rice
Chopped parsley for garnish

Preheat oven to 350 degrees F.

■ Place a pot with water on the stove and bring to a boil. Mix in 1 tablespoon salt.

■ Cut the tip of the peppers and discard seeds. Cut each pepper into 4 pieces.

■ Cut the eggplant into 1/4-inch slices. Thinly slice the zucchini, lengthwise. Cut the cauliflower head to thin "flat" flowers and cut the tip of the beans.

■ Cook the bean in the salted water for 3 minutes and remove to cold water (to halt cooking). Transfer to a plastic container.

■ Place the eggplant on a baking sheet, drizzle with olive oil and insert in the oven for 20 minutes; flip them if needed. Remove from the oven and let cool, then transfer to a plastic container.

■ Brush the zucchini and cauliflower slices with olive oil and season with salt and pepper. Heat a grilling pan or a griddle and grill the slices on both sides until fully cooked. Allow longer cooking time for

he cauliflower. Remove from the grill and let cool. Store the zucchini and cauliflower in separate plastic containers.

Prepare two marinades in separate bowls: In the first one, mix the balsamic vinegar with the extra virgin olive oil, salt and pepper, half of he garlic slices, oregano and thyme.

In the second bowl, mix the red wine vinegar, grapeseed oil, salt and pepper, the other half of the garlic slices, basil and rosemary.

■ Pour half of the first marinade over the eggplant slices and the other

half over the beans. Pour the second marinade over the cauliflower. Let the vegetables marinate for 4 hours or overnight.

■ Warm the cooked rice. Oil four small round bowls and fill each one of them with the rice. Place a serving plate over each bowl and flip. Slowly remove the bowl to uncover a dome of rice. Carefully arrange the eggplants and zucchini on the dome, alternating. Place beans and cauliflower around dome. Sprinkle with the chopped parsley and serve.

MUSHROOM & PARMESAN RISOTTO CAKES
Serves 4-6

Preparation – Mushrooms:

- Remove the stem of the mushrooms and slice them. Heat the olive oil in a wide sauté pan and sauté the shallots for two minutes; add the mushrooms and cook for 5-7 minutes over a high flame.

- Add Vermouth, thyme and cook until almost evaporated, about 3 minutes, season with salt and pepper. Remove from the pan to a strainer to get rid of excess liquids.

- Heat the stock in a large saucepan over medium heat until it comes to a boil. Reduce to a low heat, keeping the stock at a steady simmer.

- Heat the oil in heavy-bottomed saucepan over medium heat. Add the shallots, and cook until translucent, about 4 minutes. Add the rice, and cook, stirring with a wooden spoon, until the rice is coated in the oil and the kernels are translucent, about 3 minutes.

- Add the wine to the rice, and cook, stirring, until all the wine is absorbed. Ladle 3/4 cup of the hot stock into the rice, stirring constantly until most of the liquid has been absorbed, and the mixture is just thick enough to leave a clear wake when a line is drawn through it, about 3 minutes. Continue adding stock in this manner (about 3/4 cup at a time), stirring constantly, until all the stock evaporates and the rice is fully cooked and suspended in a liquid that resembles heavy cream, about 20 minutes.

- Remove risotto from heat, add cheese, mushrooms and parsley, stirring until melted and combined, about 1 minute. Season with salt, pepper and truffle oil. Let cool.

- Heat the oil to 350 degrees F and line a plate with paper towels.

- When cooled, form small balls with wet hands to prevent the risotto from sticking. Roll the balls in breadcrumbs and fry for 2 minutes until light golden and crisp. Remove from the oil to the lined plate. Serve with green salad or roasted vegetables.

8-10 cups vegetable stock
3 tablespoons extra virgin olive oil
2 large shallots, finely chopped
1 1/2 cups Arborio rice
1/2 cup dry white wine
1 cup freshly grated Parmigiano cheese
1/4 cup chopped fresh flat-leaf parsley
2 large shallots, finely minced
1 1/4 pounds (20 ounces) mixed mushrooms (cremini, button, portobello and/or shiitake)
3 tablespoons olive oil
2 tablespoons dry Vermouth
1 tablespoon fresh thyme leaves
Coarse salt and freshly ground black pepper
1 teaspoon truffle oil (optional)
Breadcrumbs
Oil for deep-frying

144

SUNNY-SIDE-UP EGG IN VEGETABLE RAGOUT
Serves 4

2 red peppers
1 onion, peeled and sliced
3 tomatoes, roughly diced
1 medium potato, peeled and sliced thinly
3 garlic cloves, minced
3 cups crushed tomatoes
Pinch of sugar
3 tablespoons olive oil
Salt and pepper
1/4 teaspoon cumin
1 teaspoon sweet paprika
4-6 eggs

■ Cut the tip of the red peppers and discard seeds, slice thinly. In a sauté pan, warm 1 tablespoon oil and sauté the onions for 1 minute until translucent. Add the peppers and garlic and sauté 3 more minutes. Add the diced tomatoes and cook for 4 minutes. Add the crushed tomatoes, sugar, salt, pepper and cumin.

■ In another big sauté pan, heat the other 2 tablespoons of oil, arrange the potato slices at the bottom of the pan, and sprinkle with the paprika. Pour the rest of the vegetables over the potatoes and cook over a medium heat for about 20 minutes, stirring with a wooden spoon to prevent the bottom of the pan from burning. Most of the liquids should evaporate, the result being a stew-like mixture.

■ Break the eggs on top of the mixture, season with salt and continue cooking until eggs are done. Serve with a slice of country bread.

VEGETARIAN STUFFED CABBAGE IN LIGHT TOMATO SAUCE

Serves 6

1 cabbage head
3/4 cup barley
1/2 cup wild rice
2 bay leaves
2 sprigs thyme
Salt and pepper
1 medium onion, diced
4 garlic cloves, crushed
1 tablespoon sweet paprika
1/2 teaspoon chili powder
2 tablespoons olive oil
1/2 cup pine nuts
6 ounces firm tofu, crumbled
1/2 cup parsley, chopped
2 tablespoons Miso paste
2 tablespoons dark brown sugar

For the Tomato sauce:
2 pounds ripe tomatoes,
blanched, peeled and diced
(with their juice)
2 cups tomato juice
1 small red onion
3 garlic cloves, crushed
1 tablespoon dark brown sugar
2 tablespoons olive oil
Salt and pepper

1/2 cup chopped chives
Parmesan cheese for garnish
(optional)

148

■ Heat a big pot with water and generously salt when boiling. Core the cabbage and cook it in the boiling water for 5 minutes. Pull leaves away as they soften. Cut out hard core of leaf. Cut largest leaves in half.

■ Cook grains in water, seasoning each with bay leaf, thyme, salt and pepper, until done. Sauté the onion and garlic in olive oil until cooked; add the spices, sugar, Miso and pine nuts and cook for two minutes. Add the cooked grains and mix well. Remove from the heat and add the tofu and parsley.

■ Sauté the garlic and onion in olive oil in a wide pot for two minutes. Add the sugar and cook for 3 more minutes. Add the tomatoes and tomato juice, season with salt and pepper and cook for 10 minutes. Taste the sauce, if too acidic add a little more sugar.

■ Fill cabbage leaves with the stuffing and wrap, tucking sides and ends in to form neat rolls. Place rolls carefully into the pot with tomato sauce. Cover and cook for 1 hour.

■ To serve, transfer stuffed cabbage to a serving plate. "Shave" the Parmesan with a peeler to achieve thin curly shaves. Sprinkle the cabbage with the chives and top with the Parmesan shavings.

SAUTÉED GREEN AND YELLOW BEANS WITH SPICED ALMONDS AND ROQUEFORT CHEESE
Serves 4-6

1 pound green beans, tips trimmed
1 pound wax (yellow) beans, tips trimmed
1 cup whole blanched almonds
1/2 teaspoon garlic powder
1/2 teaspoon onion powder
1/4 teaspoon cayenne pepper
1 tablespoon honey
2 shallots, chopped
2 garlic cloves, chopped
Salt and pepper
1/2 pound Roquefort cheese (if strong flavor is not desired substitute with a mild goat cheese)
2 tablespoons sherry wine vinegar
3 tablespoons extra virgin olive oil

Preheat the oven to 350 degrees F.

Bring a big pot with water to a boil and salt the water generously. Cook the green beans for about 3-4 minutes and remove to a bowl with ice water. Cook the yellow beans for 5 minutes and remove to a bowl with ice water.

Oil a small baking dish. Mix the almonds with the honey and season with salt, cayenne, onion and garlic powder. Transfer the almonds to the baking dish and bake for 15 minutes until golden. Let cool.

■ Heat the oil in a wide sauté pan and sauté the onion and garlic for 1 minute. Add the yellow and green beans and sauté over a high flame for 3-4 minutes. Season with salt and pepper and transfer to a big bowl. While hot, toss with the almonds, vinegar and Roquefort cheese. Serve warm.

BEET GNOCCHI IN CREAMY YOGURT SAUCE AND SAUTÉED ARUGULA

Serves 4-6

4 large Yukon gold potatoes, peeled and diced (medium)
2 medium red beets, peeled and diced (small)
1 1/2 -2 cups all purpose flour
3 egg yolks
1/2 cup Parmesan cheese (optional)
Salt and pepper

FOR THE SAUCE

2 shallots, chopped
2 garlic cloves, minced
1 ounce butter
1/2 cup white wine
11/2 cups heavy cream
1 cup good quality 4% fat yogurt
Salt and pepper
1 bunch arugula, leaves washed and dried
2 tablespoons olive oil
1 big garlic clove, sliced
1/3 cup extra virgin olive oil

■ Boil potatoes and beets in a pot of salted water until soft. Drain well, and puree in a potato ricer or food mill. Return to the puree to the dry pot and let cook over a very low heat for 5-10 minutes to dry out excess liquids (can be done in a 150 degree F preheated oven, on a baking sheet). Let cool for 15 minutes. When mixture is dry and warm add the egg yolks and gradually mix in the flour until a moist (but not sticky) dough resembling pasta dough is achieved. Season well with salt and pepper and add the Parmesan cheese.

■ Knead dough on a lightly floured surface into a ball. Cover with plastic wrap and let rest in the fridge for two hours.

■ When ready to cook, bring a big pot of water to a boil and salt the water. Cut ball into four sections and roll out each section into long, narrow strips on a lightly floured surface. Cut the strip into 3-inch pieces, using a fork to press each piece gently.

■ Cook the gnocchi in batches in the boiling water for 2 minutes, until they float. Remove to a bowl with ice water for 2 minutes and drain well.

■ Heat the butter in a wide pan and sauté the shallots and garlic for two minutes; add the wine and cook until liquid is reduced by half. Add the cream and season with salt and pepper. When the sauce starts to boil reduce the heat to low and let simmer for 5-7 minutes (the sauce should be thick). Add the gnocchi and cook for 2 more minutes. Mix in the yogurt, cook for 30 seconds and remove from the heat. In another sauté pan heat the olive oil and sauté the sliced garlic for 20 seconds; add the arugula and cook for 2 minutes. Season with salt and pepper.

■ Place the gnocchi in a deep serving plate and top with the sautéed arugula (without excess liquids). Drizzle with extra virgin olive oil and serve.

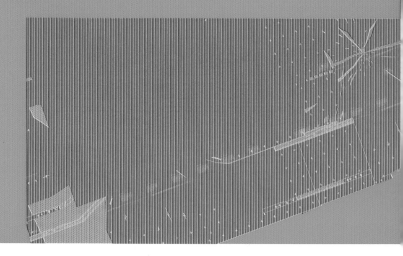

FOOD IS MUCH MORE THAN NECESSITY. IT
HAS A SOCIAL ROLE TO BRING FAMILIES
AND PEOPLE TOGETHER .

FISH

PAN-SEARED SALMON WITH CARAMELIZED PEARL ONIONS AND LENTIL RAGOUT

Serves 4

2 pounds salmon fillet	2 garlic cloves
1 tablespoon butter	1/2 cup celery, diced
6 ounces white pearl onions	1 small onion, diced
1 1/2 teaspoons sugar	1/2 cup carrots, diced
1/2 teaspoon salt	2 tablespoons balsamic vinegar
1/4 teaspoon pepper	2 stems fresh thyme
Salt and pepper	2 stems parsley
2 tablespoons olive oil	1 bay leaf
8 ounces French lentils	Salt and pepper
1 quart vegetable stock	3 tablespoons olive oil
1 tablespoon tomato paste	Cheesecloth

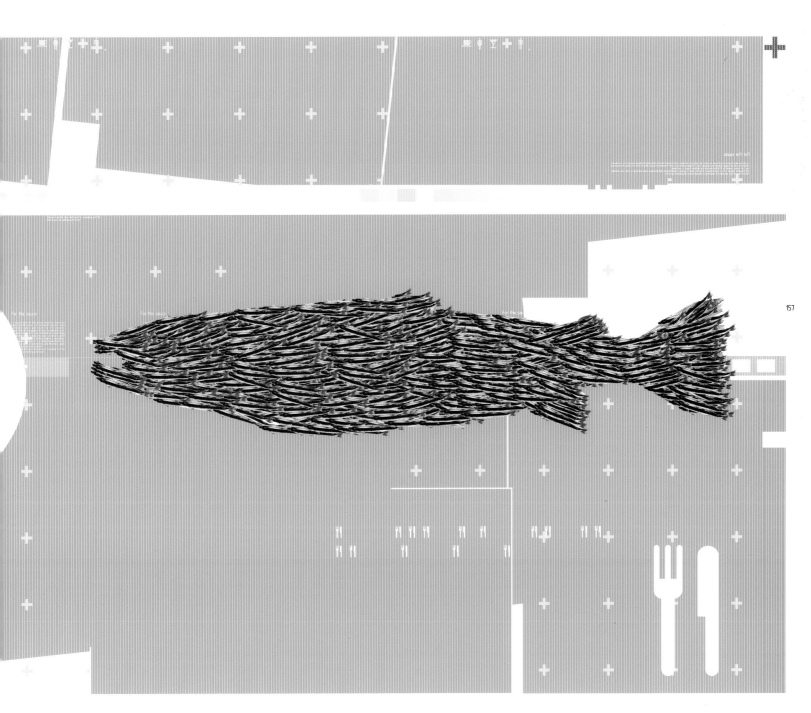

For the Caramelized Pearl Onions:

Heat the olive oil and sweat the onions, celery, carrots and garlic in a soup pot until the onions are translucent. Add the tomato paste and sauté until rust-colored. Place the herbs and bay leaves in the cheesecloth and tie. Add the stock, lentils and the cheesecloth. Simmer until the lentils are tender, about 30 minutes.

Remove and discard the cheesecloth. Add the wine, vinegar, salt and pepper. The ragout can be used immediately or stored in the refrigerator for up to a week.

To caramelize the onions, melt the butter in a large sauté pan and add onions, turning slowly and often. Add the sugar and allow the onions to glaze. Season with salt and pepper. Keep warm.

■ Cut the salmon into 8-ounce portions. Refrigerate until needed.

■ Season well with salt and pepper. Pan sear the salmon in a preheated sauté pan with 2 tablespoons olive oil until browned and cooked. If necessary, finish in a preheated oven (350 degrees F) to prevent overbrowning.

■ Place 3-4 spoons of the lentil ragout in the middle of a plate; place the salmon in the middle of the ragout and garnish with caramelized onions.

GRILLED HALIBUT WITH BRAISED ENDIVE AND BUTTERNUT SQUASH SAUCE OVER POTATO ROSTI

Serves 4

Preparation — Sauce:

■ Warm the olive oil and sweat the onions and garlic in a big pot until the onions are translucent. Add the diced butternut squash and sauté for 3-4 minutes.

■ Season with salt and pepper and add the vegetable stock. The liquids should just cover the butternut squash. Bring to a boil and reduce to medium-low heat. Let simmer covered for 35-40 minutes until the butternut squash is very tender.

■ With an emulsifier blender (or in a food processor) puree the sauce to an even, smooth texture. Add the heavy cream and bring to a boil over low heat.
Remove from the heat and taste for seasoning. Thinly slice basil leaves and mix in.

■ Cut the fish into 8-ounce portions and keep refrigerated until needed.

Preparation — Braised Endives:

■ Slice the endives 1/4-inch thick, lengthwise, keeping the shape of the endive. Pour 3 tablespoons water in a 12-inch sauté pan; arrange the endive slices (do not crowd the pan) and sprinkle with 3 tablespoons brown sugar. Bring to a quick boil then reduce to a very

2 pounds halibut fillet
4 endives
3+3 tablespoons dark brown sugar
3+3 tablespoons water
1 small butternut squash, peeled, seeded and diced 1/2 inch thick
1 medium onion, diced
4 garlic cloves, chopped
1 cup heavy cream
2 tablespoons olive oil
3-4 cups vegetable stock or water
10 basil leaves, washed and dried
7 Idaho potatoes
1/2 cup vegetable oil
Salt and pepper

ow heat and cover. Let cook for about 10 minutes until the "heart" of he endive slices are soft and the color is light brown. Remove from the an and cook another batch if needed. Keep warm.

Preparation — Rosti:

Peel and grate the potatoes (can be done in a food processor). Place handfuls in a towel and squeeze to remove excess liquids; place in a ew mixing bowl and repeat with the remaining potatoes. Season the otatoes well with salt and pepper.

Heat the oil in two nonstick pans until hot, but not smoking. Layer he potatoes evenly in the pans (not thicker than 1/2 inch) and cook over medium heat for 5-7 minutes until the rosti is fully cooked. With the help of a plate or a flat tray flip the rosti to the other side (add a little more oil if needed) and cook for an additional 7 minutes. Remove from the heat and keep warm.

■ Heat a grilling pan, or griddle. Brush the fish lightly with olive oil and season with salt and pepper. Grill skin side up for 3-4 minutes then flip sides and grill for 4-5 additional minutes. Cooking can be finished in a preheated oven (375 degrees F).

■ Slice the rosti into thin triangles with a knife or pizza wheel to create 2 per servings. Place the triangles in a serving plate, overlap 4 slices of the endive on the plate and top with the fish. Ladle the sauce around and serve.

ROASTED RED SNAPPER WITH ORANGE-ROSEMARY FLAVORS
Serves 4-6

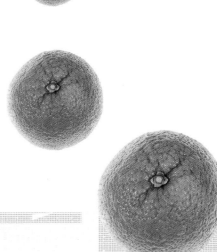

3 pounds whole snapper
2 oranges
2 garlic cloves, chopped.
1 stem fresh rosemary, leaves only
Salt and pepper
1 cup orange juice
3 shallots, chopped
1 cup white wine
3 cups Basmati rice
2/3 cup currants
1 teaspoon saffron
1/2 teaspoon cayenne pepper
2 tablespoons olive oil
4 1/2 cups water
Salt and pepper

@　#　%　&　*　@　#　+　(　^

Preheat oven to 375 degrees F.

Grate the oranges. Place the zest in a small baking pan on top of the stove, where it is warm but there is no direct heat.

Heat the olive oil in a saucepan; add the shallots and saute for 2 minutes; add the wine and cook for 5 minutes. Add half of the garlic, orange juice and 5 rosemary leaves. Season with salt and pepper and let cook for 5 minutes. Remove from the heat.

Thinly slice one orange. Line a baking dish with the slices; set aside 3 slices. Place the fish on top the orange slices. Stuff the fish with the 3 remaining slices and the garlic. Season with salt and pepper and sprinkle with the rosemary leaves. Puree 1/2 cup of the orange sauce and bake on the top oven shelf for 15 minutes. Remove pan from oven and flip the fish onto the other side gently. Bake for 10 minutes. If needed add liquids to the pan.

■ While the fish is cooking heat the oil in a pot and sauté the rice briefly, about 30 seconds. Add 4 1/2 cups of water, saffron and 1 teaspoon salt. Bring to a boil; reduce to low heat and cover. Let cook undisturbed for 20 minutes or until liquids are gone and the rice is ready. Remove the cover and let stand off the heat for 5 minutes. Transfer to a mixing bowl and mix in the cayenne pepper and currants gently.

■ Serve the fish with the rice and the leftover sauce. Sprinkle the rice or the fish with the dried orange zest.

GRILLED SEA BASS OVER BAKED SWEET POTATOES AND SAUTÉED SPINACH IN RED WINE SAUCE

Serves 4

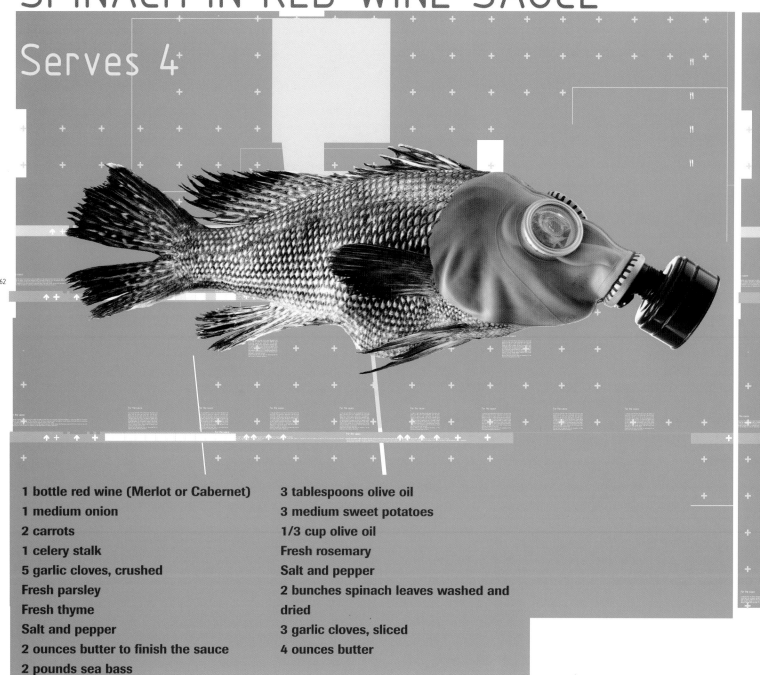

1 bottle red wine (Merlot or Cabernet)	3 tablespoons olive oil
1 medium onion	3 medium sweet potatoes
2 carrots	1/3 cup olive oil
1 celery stalk	Fresh rosemary
5 garlic cloves, crushed	Salt and pepper
Fresh parsley	2 bunches spinach leaves washed and
Fresh thyme	dried
Salt and pepper	3 garlic cloves, sliced
2 ounces butter to finish the sauce	4 ounces butter
2 pounds sea bass	

Preheat oven to 375 degrees F.

Preparation – Sauce:

■ Slice the onion, carrots and celery. Heat 2 tablespoons of olive oil in a saucepot and sauté the vegetables for 2 minutes. Add the wine and herbs and bring to a boil. Reduce to a low heat and let reduce by three quarters. Strain and set aside for use later.

■ Slice the sweet potatoes, thinly. Overlap them in a baking pan, drizzle with olive oil, season with salt and pepper, and sprinkle with fresh rosemary. Cover with foil and place in the oven. Bake for 30 minutes then remove foil and bake for an additional 15-20 minutes.

■ Score the skin side of the fish lightly.

■ Brush the fish fillets with olive oil and season with salt and pepper. Heat a grilling pan or a griddle until very hot and place the fish flesh side down on the pan. Grill for 1 minute and turn 90 degrees to create a crisscross mark. Grill another minute and flip to the skin side for 2 minutes. Cooking can be finished in a preheated oven.

■ Melt the butter in a sauté pan, sauté the garlic for 30 seconds, and add the spinach. Season with salt and pepper and cook for 1 minute.

Remove from the heat.

■ To finish the sauce, heat a sauté pan and pour in the reduced wine allowing to boil for 20 seconds. Add 2 ounces of butter, mixing constantly, until the sauce thickens and has a rich texture.

■ Arrange 6 slices of the sweet potatoes; place the fish on top, followed by the spinach, and drizzle around with sauce.

PAN-SEARED TILAPIA OVER PEAR AND MINT RISOTTO IN BALSAMIC REDUCTION SAUCE AND GRILLED SCALLIONS

Serves 4

4 6-8 ounce tilapia fillets
2 ounces butter or olive oil
1 small onion, diced
2 garlic cloves, minced
2 ounces butter
2 cups Arborio rice
1/2 cup dry white wine
1 1/2 quarts vegetable stock
1/2 cup pear nectar

3 pears peeled and diced
1/2 cup chopped mint leaves
Salt and pepper
1 bottle good balsamic vinegar
2 shallots, chopped
8 scallions
1 tablespoon olive oil
Salt and pepper

■ Heat the oil in a high saucepan and sauté the chopped shallots for 2 minutes. Add the balsamic vinegar, bring to a boil and reduce to a simmer. Let cook until the balsamic is thick enough to coat the back of a spoon (about 25 minutes) and reduced by two thirds. Keep warm.

■ In a big wide pot, melt the butter and sauté the onions and garlic for 2 minutes. Add the rice and the white wine mixing constantly. When liquids are gone add 1 cup of the vegetable stock at a time, mixing until liquids are reduced. Continue until rice is fully cooked about 20-25 minutes. Add the pears and the mint, followed by the pear nectar. Season well with salt and

pepper and cook for 5 additional minutes. Remove from the heat and keep warm.

■ Brush the scallions with the olive oil and season well with salt and pepper. Grill in a grill pan or over a griddle for 2-3 minutes on each side. Keep in a warm place to continue cooking (can be done in a 350 degrees F preheated oven).

■ Season the fish well and sauté in the butter, in a preheated sauté pan, 3 minutes on each side. Place 3-4 tablespoons of the risotto in the middle of a serving plate and top with the fish. Drizzle around with balsamic reduction sauce and place 2 scallions in an X over the fish.

BRAISED SALMON IN TOMATO STEW OVER CRISPY POLENTA AND YOUNG LEAVES SALAD

Serves 4

4 8-ounce salmon fillets

8 high quality tomatoes, poached, peeled and diced

4 garlic cloves, sliced

1 medium yellow onion, sliced

1/2 cup sun dried tomatoes in oil, drained

1 small string fresh rosemary1/2 cup Nicoise olives, pitted

1 teaspoon sugar

1/2 teaspoon ground cumin

2 tablespoons olive oil

1/2 cup fresh basil leaves juliennes

3 1/3 cups vegetable stock

4 cups whole milk

Preparation — Tomato Stew:

■ Heat the olive oil in a medium sized saucepan, add the onion, garlic and sun dried tomatoes and sauté 2-3 minutes until onion is translucent. Add the cumin and olives and cook for 2 more minutes. Add the tomatoes, sugar, salt, pepper and rosemary. Lower the heat and cook, covered for 45 minutes. Add the salmon fillet and cook covered for 7-10 minutes to the internal temperature desired. Add the basil before serving.

Preparation — Polenta:

■ Combine the stock and milk in a large saucepan. Season with salt and pepper, and bring to a boil over high heat. Stir in the polenta. Reduce the heat and continue stirring with a wooden spoon for about

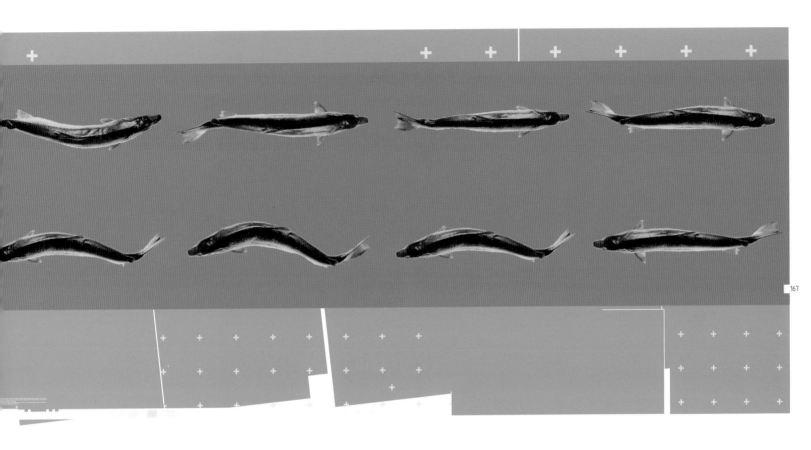

Salt and fresh ground white pepper to taste

2 cups instant polenta

1/2 cup grated Parmesan cheese

3 tablespoons olive oil

1/2 cup young celery leaves

1/2 cup young parsley leaves

1/3 cup young mint leaves

1/3 cup young basil leaves

1/3 cup chives cut quarter inch long

1 tablespoon extra virgin olive oil

2 teaspoons lemon juice

5 minutes, or until the polenta is smooth and pulls away from the sides of the pan.

■ Pour into two sheet pans, so that the polenta is about half-inch thick. Cool, cover with plastic wrap and refrigerate.

■ When polenta has solidified, about 20-30 minutes later, flip out of the pan and onto a cutting board, with the plastic wrap acting as a protective layer. Cut out circles or squares with a knife or cookie cutter.

■ When ready to serve, heat the olive oil in a nonstick pan and sauté the polenta 2 minutes on each side until crispy. Mix all the young leaves in a bowl with the lemon juice, olive oil and salt.

■ Place 2 portions of the polenta in the middle of a serving plate with the salmon on top and surround with some of the stew (using a spoon). Top with the young leaves salad and serve.

FILLET OF SOLE IN BROWN SAGE AND CAPERS BUTTER OVER WHITE BEAN PUREE AND SAUTÉED ARUGULA

Serves 4

For the sauce:

Place the lemon zest in a small baking sheet or pan in a hot place (on top of the stove) or in a 120 degree F preheated oven for about 1-2 hours until dry.

Preparation — White Bean Puree

■ Place the beans, water, garlic and onion in a pot. Bring to a boil and discard the white foam. Lower to medium/low heat, add the herbs and season well with salt and pepper. Cook covered until beans are very soft (about 45-60 minutes). Remove the herbs and drain, letting the beans sit in the colander for 5 minutes. Puree, using a food mill or a food processor. If using a food processor puree for a short time to avoid sticky texture. Check for seasoning.

■ In a heated, nonstick pan, add 1 ounce of butter. Season the fish with salt and pepper and cook for 1-2 minutes on each side. Remove the fish from the pan and add the rest of the butter.

When fully melted, add the sage and capers (be careful, wet capers will cause butter to splatter). Cook until butter turns brown.

■ Place 3 tablespoons of the white bean puree on the side of a serving plate, lean fillet of sole against it and drizzle with the butter sauce. Cook the chopped garlic in a buttered pan for 30 seconds, add the arugula and season with salt. Cook for 1 minute until arugula is cooked (this can be done in advance and arugula can be quickly reheated). Place on top of the fish and serve.

For the sauce:

For the sauce:

For the sauce:

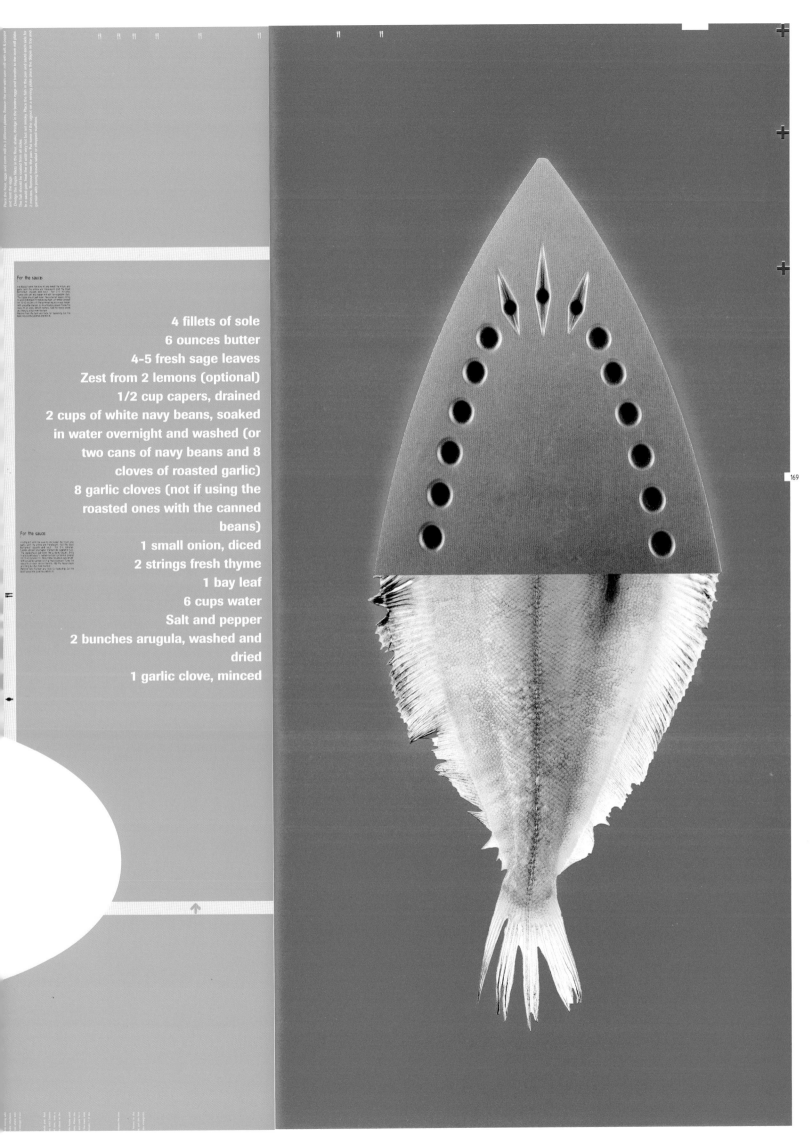

For the sauce:

4 fillets of sole
6 ounces butter
4-5 fresh sage leaves
Zest from 2 lemons (optional)
1/2 cup capers, drained
2 cups of white navy beans, soaked
in water overnight and washed (or
two cans of navy beans and 8
cloves of roasted garlic)
8 garlic cloves (not if using the
roasted ones with the canned
beans)
1 small onion, diced
2 strings fresh thyme
1 bay leaf
6 cups water
Salt and pepper
2 bunches arugula, washed and
dried
1 garlic clove, minced

SAUTEED RED SNAPPER FILLET WITH SPICE RUB OVER LIMA BEANS IN TOMATO VINAIGRETTE
Serves 4

4 fillets of red snapper (6-7 ounces each)
2 garlic cloves
1 teaspoon ground cumin
1/2 teaspoon ground cardamom
1/4 teaspoon cinnamon
1/4 teaspoon ground fresh pepper
Pinch of ground cloves
2 tablespoons olive oil
2 ounces butter or olive oil
2 pounds Lima beans, frozen and thawed

3 garlic cloves, crushed
3 tablespoons olive oil
2/3 cup olives, chopped
2 tomatoes, poached, peeled, seeded and pureed
1 clove garlic
1/2 cup balsamic vinegar
1 cup olive oil
Salt and pepper to taste

Preparation – Rub:

Crush the garlic cloves and mix with the spices using the back of spoon (pressing constantly to create a paste). Add the oil slowly while mixing until texture is smooth. Score the skin side of each fish and rub the meat side with the spice rub. Season with salt and refrigerate.

Preparation – Vinaigrette:

Puree tomatoes in a blender. Add garlic and vinegar and blend again. Transfer to mixing bowl and slowly whisk oil into mixture. Taste for flavor. If too sharp add more oil: if too mild add more vinegar.

■ Heat olive oil in a sauté pan. Add lima beans and garlic; toss until beans are cooked but still firm, only a few minutes. Toss in olives at the last minute.

■ Heat the butter in a sauté pan until very hot but not smoky; place the fish skin side down and cook for 2 minutes then flip to the meat side and cook 2 more minutes. If the pan is not hot enough skin will stick to the pan.

To Assemble:

■ Place some of the beans in the middle of each plate, top with the fish and drizzle the vinaigrette around the beans.

STEAMED TROUT IN GRAPE LEAVES WITH BLACK OLIVE PASTE, TOMATOES AND GARLIC OVER SAFFRON COUSCOUS AND ARUGULA OIL

Serves 4

4 trouts, insides cleaned
1 jar grape leaves
12 garlic cloves
2 tomatoes, sliced
1 pound black olives, pitted
1 8-ounce box couscous
3 cups water
Pinch saffron
Salt and pepper
1 tablespoon olive oil
1 bunch arugula
2 cups olive oil

Preheat oven to 375 degrees F.

■ Put the garlic cloves in a foil and place in the oven. Bake for 15 minutes.

■ Wash and dry the arugula, then blend well with the 2 cups olive oil. Transfer to a squeeze bottle.

■ Wash the grape leaves in water and dry them. Puree the black olives in a food processor (add capers and or/anchovies for flavor).

■ Clean the stomach cavity of the fish and season with salt and pepper. Spread a thin layer of the black olive paste and stuff with 2-3 slices of tomatoes and 3 garlic cloves. Season the fish's skin with salt and pepper. Overlap 2-3 grape leaves and wrap the fish. Place the fish in the oven and bake for 20 minutes.

■ Bring the water and saffron to a boil. In a mixing bowl, season the couscous with salt and pepper and toss lightly with the oil. Pour the saffron water over the couscous to cover, wrap with plastic wrap and place in a warm place for 10 minutes. Remove the plastic wrap, mix the couscous and wrap again for 5 minutes.

■ Place the couscous in the middle of a serving plate, lean the fish against it and drizzle with arugula oil

SAUTÉED RED MULLET OVER FORBIDDEN BLACK RICE AND ROASTED ASPARAGUS IN CITRUS REDUCTION SAUCE

Serves 4

12 red mullet fillets (about 2 ounces
each, 3 fillets per serving)
2 tablespoons olive oil
2 cups forbidden black rice or wild rice
4 cups vegetable or chicken stock
1 stem fresh sage
3 cups fresh tangerine juice
2 cups fresh orange juice
2 shallots, chopped
2 garlic cloves, minced
2 tablespoons olive oil
1/2 teaspoon fennel seeds
1/2 teaspoon whole white pepper
2 kefir lime leaves
2 stems fresh thyme
1/2 Star anise
Cheesecloth
Segments from 2 oranges
2 bunches asparagus
2 tablespoons extra virgin olive oil
1 teaspoon fresh thyme leaves
Salt and pepper

Preheat oven to 375 degrees F.

■ Cook the rice in the vegetable stock with the sage in a covered pot, over low heat, until the liquid has dried up and rice is tender (about 50-60 minutes).

■ Place all the aromatics and herbs for the sauce in the cheesecloth and tie well. Pour olive oil in a big pan and sauté the garlic and shallots for 1 minute. Add the citrus juice and cheesecloth and lower the heat. Reduce by half and season with salt and pepper. Remove the cheesecloth and keep warm.

■ Cut the root end of the asparagus (about half inch) and peel them from the middle down. Brush with olive oil and place on a baking sheet; sprinkle with the thyme leaves and roast in the oven for 15 minutes.

■ Season the fish with salt and pepper and sauté in a big pan with the olive oil for 1 to 2 minutes on each side. Place about 5 asparagus per person in a plate and top with 3-4 tablespoons rice. Lean the red mullet fillets, with the tail side up, against the rice. Drizzle with the sauce and garnish with a few orange segments.

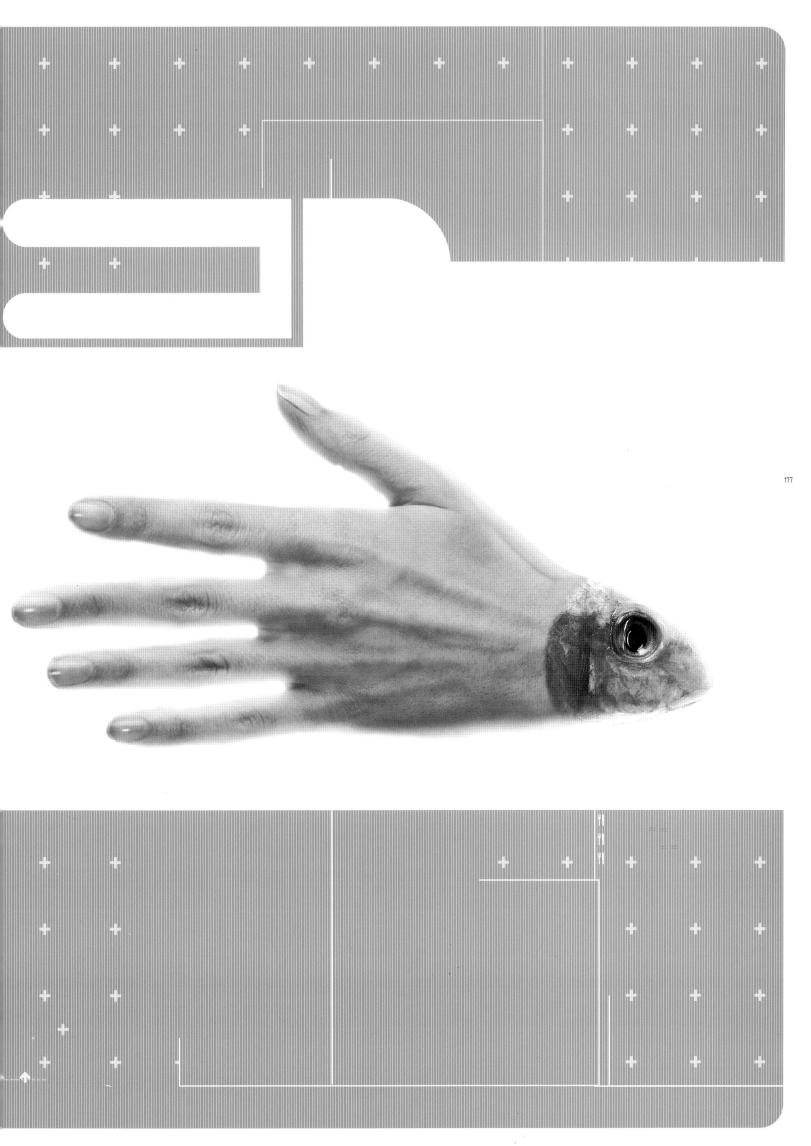

WASABI PEA-CRUSTED TUNA STEAKS WITH GREEN PEA PUREE AND MISO CARROT SAUCE

Serves 4

4 7-ounce high quality tuna steaks

1 package Wasabi crusted peas

1 egg, beaten

3 tablespoons peanut oil or vegetable oil

1 pound fresh green peas (or frozen and thawed)

1 Idaho potato, peeled and diced

1 tablespoon cilantro leaves, chopped

4 tablespoons olive oil or 1/3 cup heavy cream

Juice from 1/2 lemon

Salt and pepper

2 medium carrots, peeled and sliced

2 cups fresh (unsweetened) carrot juice

1-2 tablespoons light brown (Japanese) miso paste

1/2 teaspoon chopped fresh ginger

1 garlic clove, minced

1 tablespoon peanut oil or vegetable oil

■ Heat the peanut oil in a medium saucepan and sauté the garlic for 20 seconds. Add the carrot and ginger and cook for 2 minutes. Add the carrot juice and 1 tablespoon miso and taste. If needed add another tablespoon miso paste. (The sauce should not be too salty!) Cook, uncovered, over medium heat for 30 minutes until carrots are very soft. Purée to a smooth texture and check for flavor. If the sauce is too thick add a little carrot juice or water.

■ Cook the potato dices and the fresh peas in boiling salted water until very soft, about 20 minutes. If using frozen peas, cook the potato for 10 minutes and then add the thawed peas for 10 more minutes.

■ Strain well and transfer to a food processor with the olive oil. Puree, pressing the pulse button to get to the wanted consistency. Add the lemon juice and mix in. Taste for flavor and season as needed. If too dry add a little more olive oil. Keep warm until serving.

■ Crush the Wasabi-crusted peas in a food processor for 15 seconds. Dip one side of the tuna steaks in the beaten egg and season with salt. Dip the egg-dipped side of the tuna in the Wasabi crust. Heat the oil in a sauté pan and place the tuna steaks, crust side down, in the pan. Cook for 2 minutes; gently flip sides and cook 2 more minutes. For more than a medium rare temperature, finish the cooking process in a preheated oven (375 degrees F).

■ Place some of the puree in a middle of a plate, top with the tuna and drizzle around with sauce.

GROUPER FILLETS OVER EGGPLANT CAVIAR, WARM BALSAMIC VINAIGRETTE AND POTATO SHOE STRINGS

Serves 4

Preparation — Caviar:

■ Poke the eggplants with a fork. Roast the eggplants over the stove or a grill, turning them every few minutes, until the skin is lightly burnt and the eggplants are very soft (about 15 minutes each). Remove from the heat and place in a colander in the sink to get rid of excess liquids and cool.

■ When cooled, but still warm, peel the skin off using your hands or a small knife. Save a small piece of the burnt skin. Puree 2/3 of the eggplant, garlic, oil and lemon juice in a blender and season well with salt and pepper. Correct seasoning as needed. Add the parsley the remaining eggplant, the saved burnt eggplant skin and th Tabasco and puree for a short time so the final texture will be a littl chunky. Keep warm.

Preparation — Vinaigrette:

■ Sauté the shallot in 1 tablespoon of the olive oil for 1 minute, unt translucent. Add the balsamic vinegar and honey; lower the hea

4 8-ounce grouper fillets

2 tablespoons olive oil

2 medium firm eggplants

1/4 cup extra virgin olive oil

2 garlic cloves

Juice of 1 lemon

1/2 cup parsley leaves, washed and dried

1/2 teaspoon Tabasco sauce (optional)

1/3 cup high quality balsamic vinegar

1 cup extra virgin olive oil

1 shallot, chopped

1 teaspoon honey

Salt and Pepper

2 Idaho potatoes

Canola oil, enough for deep-frying

and mix well until the honey fully dissolves. Transfer to a mixing bowl and while whisking add the olive oil very slowly for a thick texture. Season with salt and pepper and check for flavor. If too bland add a little more balsamic. Keep in a dish of warm water.

■ Peel the potatoes and slice thinly, lengthwise. Cut slices like strings (use a mandolin if you have one). Heat the oil to 350 degrees F. Deep-fry the potato strings until golden and crisp. Do not overcrowd the frying pot; fry in two batches, if needed. Transfer potatoes to plate lined with paper towels using a slotted spoon. Sprinkle with salt.

■ Season the fish with salt and pepper. Heat the oil in a sauté pan and cook the fish for about 3-4 minutes on each side. Place 3 tablespoons of the eggplant caviar in the middle of a serving plate and arrange the fish on top. Top with the fried potato strings and drizzle around with the warm vinaigrette. Serve immediately.

PAN-SEARED TILAPIA WITH CORNMEAL CRUST OVER LEEKS, RED PEPPERS AND POTATO RAGOUT

Serves 4

4 Tilapia fillets
1 package cornmeal
2 eggs
Flour
1/3 cup oil
2 leeks
3 red peppers
4 medium Yukon gold potatoes or
Idaho potatoes
6-8 cups vegetable stock
Salt and pepper
Fresh thyme

Preparation

■ Place the flour, eggs and cornmeal in 3 different plates. Season the cornmeal with salt and pepper. Beat the eggs.

■ Dredge the tilapia fillets in the flour, shake, dredge in the beaten eggs and transfer to the cornmeal plate. The fish should be thoroughly coated.

■ Pour oil in a sauté pan (oil should be very hot but not smoky). Place the fish in the pan and sauté each side for 2 minutes. Remove from the pan. Place some of the ragout on a serving plate with the tilapia on top and garnish with young leaves salad or chopped scallions.

Preparation – Ragout:

■ Place the oil in a pot and heat up. Put the red pepper in the pot and sauté for 2-3 minutes until slightly brown.

■ Add the leeks and stir together.

■ Place the potatoes inside the pot, and stir together and cook for 2-3 minutes.

■ Add vegetable stock and the thyme and cook on low heat until potatoes are soft, but not falling a part.

■ Season with salt and pepper and keep it in a warm place until served.

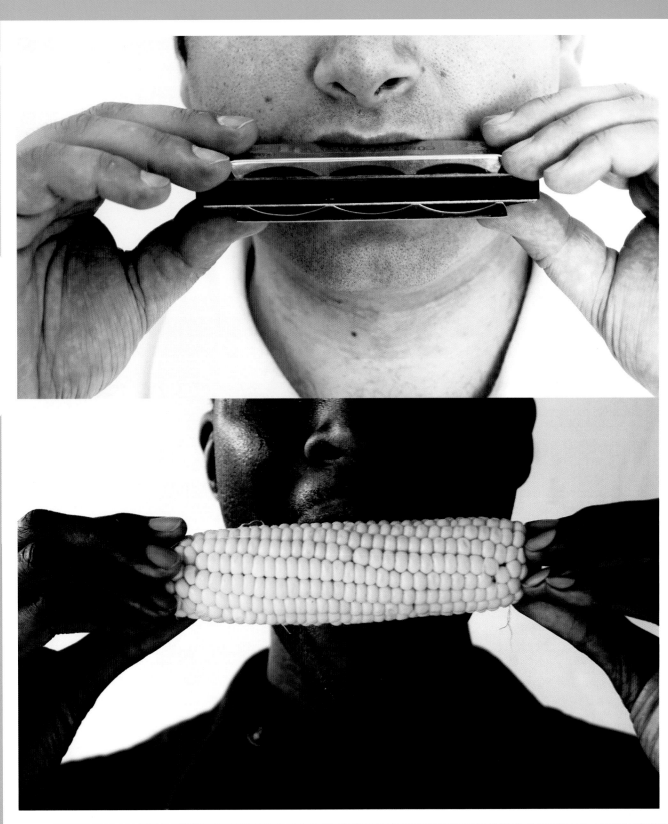

STEAMED CHILEAN SEA BASS IN GINGER AND MISO BROTH OVER RAMEN NOODLES WITH CRISPY WONTON SKINS

Serves 4

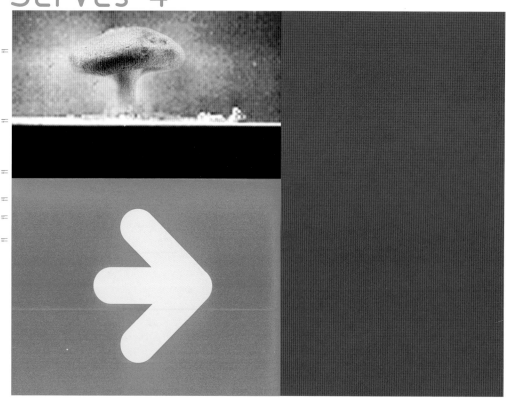

2 pounds Chilean sea bass

4 tablespoons light brown Miso paste

3 ounces fresh ginger, peeled and sliced thinly

1 romaine lettuce

5 garlic cloves, sliced

5 scallions, washed and sliced (white part included)

1 bunch fresh spinach, washed and dried

6 cups water or stock (vegetable, chicken)

1 box Ramen noodles

1/3 cup soy sauce

1/2 package Wonton skins (for frying)

8 ounces dried shiitake

Norri seaweed

3 cups hot water

Oil for deep-frying and 2 tablespoons peanut oil

1 tablespoon sesame oil

sal and pepper

■ Place the dried shiitake in a mixing bowl and cover with hot water. Let stand for 10 minutes. Sauté the white part of the scallions, garlic and ginger for 2 minutes. Add the water and miso paste; stir well until miso fully dissolves and add soy sauce. Cook for 10 minutes. Strain the shiitake mushrooms from the water and slice each in four. Add to the broth.

■ Bring the frying oil to 375 degrees F. Thinly slice the wonton skins and fry, carefully, in small batches, until golden and crispy. Remove from the oil to a plate lined with paper towels.

■ Cook the ramen noodles as directed on the package. Keep warm.

■ Line a steaming dish with the romaine lettuce. Cut the fish into 8-ounce portions; season with salt and pepper and place on the lettuce. Steam for about 15 minutes.

■ Five minutes before serving, add the spinach and the green part of the scallion to the broth. Add the sesame oil and check for flavor. Add more miso paste or liquids as needed.

■ Pour some of the broth in a soup bowl and place a handful of the noodles in the middle of the plate with the fish on top. Garnish with pieces of the Norri seaweed and the fried wonton skin.

CRISPY BLACK BASS WITH FENNEL JAM AND SAFFRON VINAIGRETTE
Serves 4

4 8-ounce fillets of black bass
2 heads of fennel, sliced 1/4–inch thick
2 cups fresh orange juice +additional 1/2 cup
1/4 cup honey
1/2 cup currants
Kosher salt and freshly ground black pepper
1/2 teaspoon saffron threads
6 tablespoons extra virgin olive oil
1 1/2 tablespoons champagne vinegar
1/4 cup finely chopped flat-leaf parsley
Extra virgin olive oil, for drizzling

■ Combine the fennel, orange juice (minus the pulp), honey, and currants in a shallow, heavy-bottomed pan and simmer over low heat until the liquid is reduced by half and the fennel is very tender, about 30 minutes. Drain the fennel, season with salt and pepper and set aside to cool.

■ Place the 1/2 cup orange juice in a small, stainless sti▮ saucepan and warm over medium heat until its juices are released, adding water, if necessary, to prevent scorching. Add the saffron, cover and turn off the heat. Combine the saffron and orange juice mixture with 4 tablespoons of the olive oil, the champagne vinegar, salt and pepper and whisk well for a thick▮

2 lb tuna
1 small onion, chopped
2 garlic cloves, minced
3 tablespoon olive oil
1 tablespoon soy sauce
1 teaspoon sesame oil (optional)
cup chopped parsley
Salt & pepper

Burger buns
Mayo
Tomato, sliced
Iceberg lettuce

2 medium onions
Wondra flour
Oil for dip frying

texture. Set aside.

■ Heat the remaining 2 tablespoons of olive oil in a big sauté pan over high heat until smoking. Score the skin of each fish fillet twice and season well with salt and pepper. Place in a pan, skin side down and cook until crispy on the skin side, about 3 minutes. Turn and finish cooking on the flesh side, about 2 more minutes.

■ Meanwhile, in a sauté pan, heat the fennel jam over high heat until warmed through. Stir in the parsley. Place one portion of the jam on each of four dinner plates. Place a fillet on top, spoon vinaigrette around, and drizzle with the oil. Serve immediately.

BAKED CODSTEAKS OVER CHICKPEA PANCAKES IN ROASTED GARLIC AND GRILLED TOMATO SAUCE

Serves 4

4 seven-ounce cod steaks
2 garlic heads
8 ripe tomatoes
1 small onion
2 stems fresh thyme
1 stem fresh rosemary

1/2 cup chopped fresh parsley leaves
2 bay leaves
2+2 tablespoons olive oil
2 cups chickpea flour
1 teaspoon salt
1/2 teaspoon ground cumin

1/4 teaspoon cayenne pepper
1/2 teaspoon turmeric powder
11/2 cups water
Vegetable oil to coat frying pan

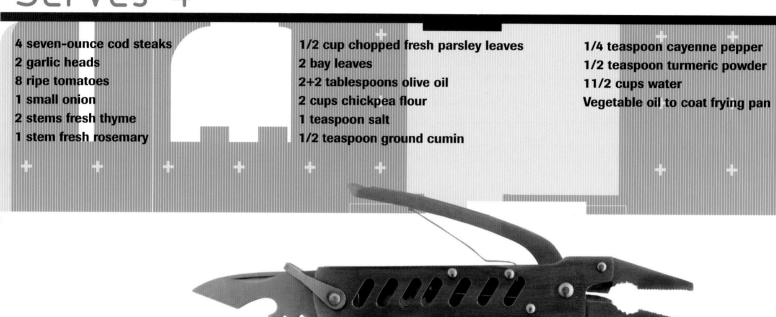

Preheat oven to 375 degrees F.

Peel the garlic, place in aluminum foil, drizzle with olive oil and bake for 30 minutes until the cloves are very tender. Grill 6 tomatoes in a hot grilling pan on all sides, about 5 minutes.

Peel and dice the onion. Heat 2 tablespoons olive oil in a saucepan, add the onion and sauté for 2 minutes. Add the tomatoes, bay leaves and 1 thyme stem and cook for 10 minutes over medium heat. Season with salt and pepper. Discard the bay leaves and thyme stem and puree the sauce in a food processor. Add the garlic and process for 2 minutes; strain the sauce.

While the sauce is cooking season the fish steaks with salt and pepper. Slice the remaining 2 tomatoes and line a baking sheet with the slices. Place fish on top of the tomatoes and sprinkle with fresh thyme and rosemary leaves. Cover with aluminum foil and bake for 15-20 minutes.

Preparation – Chickpea Pancakes:

■ Mix all dry ingredients together in a food processor or bowl. Add 1 1/2 cups water and blend well. Use a large serving spoon to drop mixture into oiled frying pan. Fry on both sides over a medium flame about 1 to 2 minutes, or until golden brown. Keep warm.

■ Place pancakes on a serving plate with the fish next to the pancake and top with the sauce. Garnish with the chopped parsley leaves.

189

TUNA BURGERS WITH ONION RINGS
Serves 4

2 pounds tuna
1 small onion, chopped
2 garlic cloves, minced
3 tablespoons olive oil
1 tablespoon soy sauce
1 teaspoon sesame oil (optional)
1/2 cup chopped parsley
Salt and pepper
Burger buns
Mayonnaise
Tomato, sliced
Iceberg lettuce
2 medium onions
Wondra flour
Oil for deep-frying

■ Cut the tuna into small dices and mix with the rest of the ingredients. Season with salt and pepper.

■ Heat 1/4 cup of oil in a big sauté pan. Form 4 burgers from the seasoned tuna "throwing" them from one hand to the other to "punch" the air out. Place them in the pan and sauté 3 minutes on each side. For well-done burgers, finish the cooking in a preheated oven.

■ Heat the frying oil to 350 degrees F.
■ Slice the onions thinly on a mandolin or with a sharp knife. In a mixing bowl, toss them with the Wondra flour then get rid of excess flour. Place the onion slices in the oil and fry them for 1 minute until lightly golden. Transfer to a plate lined with paper towel and sprinkle them with salt.

■ Serve on a burger bun with mayo, tomato and lettuce while hot, with onion rings on the side, or placed on top

LEARN TO LOVE FOOD BY TRYING NEW
THINGS. BE CURIOUS.

POULTRY

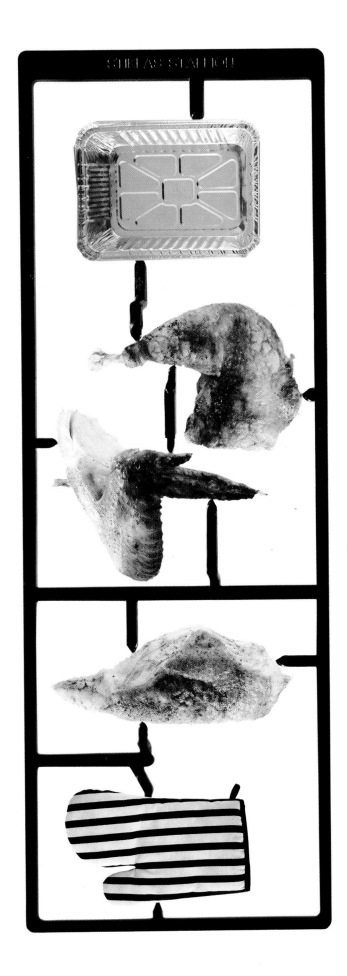

MAPLE AND GARLIC ROASTED CHICKEN OVER HERBED PANCAKE AND SAUTÉED BROCCOLI RABE

Serves 4

3 pounds chicken, quartered
Salt and pepper
1/2 cup Hoi Sin sauce
1/3 cup Canola oil
2/3 cup maple syrup
12 garlic cloves, peeled
1/2 cup white wine or chicken stock
2 tablespoons Miso paste

For the pancake:
8 ounces cake flour
1 teaspoon salt
1 tablespoon baking powder

2 large eggs
2 cups soy milk
2 tablespoons chopped parsley
2 tablespoons chopped mint
1 tablespoon chopped sage
2 ounces margarine, melted
1/2 cup olive oil

1 large bunch broccoli rabe
2 tablespoons extra virgin olive oil
2 large garlic cloves, smashed and cut into thin slices
Coarse salt and freshly ground black pepper

Preheat oven to 375 degrees F.

- Using your hands, rub the Hoi Sin sauce under the skin of the chicken, gently, to avoid tearing. Season the chicken parts with salt and pepper.

- Heat the oil in a wide sauté pan and sear the chicken for 3-4 minutes on each side, until golden and crisp. Remove to a baking dish.

- Add the wine to the pan and scorch the bottom with a wooden spoon. Add the maple, Miso and garlic cloves. Taste for flavor. If too sweet, add a little more wine and Miso; if too salty, add a little more maple syrup. Season with salt and pepper

- Pour the sauce over the chicken parts and cover with aluminum foil. Bake in oven for 45 minutes; remove the foil and bake 15-20 additional minutes.

Preparation – Pancake:

- In a mixing bowl combine flour, salt and baking powder.

Mix well.
- In a second bowl combine milk, eggs and margarine. Mix well. Add the liquid ingredients to the dry ingredients and mix until combined. Add the herbs, DON'T OVERMIX.

- Heat a non-stick pan and grease it lightly with olive oil. With a two-ounce ladle, measure portions of the pancake batter onto the pan. Fry the pancakes until the tops are full of bubbles and begin to look dry. Turn and brown the other side.

- Trim 2 inches off the bottom of the broccoli rabe stalks, and discard. In a large skillet, heat the olive oil over medium heat. Add the garlic slices and cook until fragrant and lightly golden, about 20 seconds. Add the broccoli rabe and sauté until it is coated in the garlic oil, about 2 minutes. Season with salt.

- Place 2 pancakes on each serving plate, place one of the chicken parts on top and drizzle with sauce. Top with the broccoli rabe and serve.

CRISPY DUCK BREAST WITH MANGO RELISH AND YUCCA FRIES
Serves 4

4 duck breasts with skin, about 8 ounces each
3 mangoes, ripe but not too soft
1 small red onion, diced small
1 garlic clove, minced
1 teaspoon chopped fresh ginger
3 tablespoons light brown sugar
1/2 teaspoon curry powder
1/2 teaspoon cayenne pepper
2 tablespoons lime juice
2 tablespoons extra virgin olive oil
1/2 cup chopped mint leaves
11/2 pounds yucca
Vegetable oil for deep-frying
Salt and pepper

■ Peel the mangoes, cut the fruit around the pit and dice to one-eighth of an inch. Place in a big mixing bowl and mix with the rest of the ingredients. Check for flavor. If too spicy add more sugar.

Heat the frying oil to 350 degrees F.
■ Peel the yucca and slice, paper thin, on a mandolin or with a very sharp knife. Fry in batches until golden and crisp. Transfer to a plate lined with paper towel and season with salt while hot.

■ Score the duck fat (skin) with a sharp knife. Heat a heavy pan and place the duck, skin side down to melt the fat, about 10 minutes over medium heat. Remove the

breasts, season with salt and pepper and get rid of the excess fat (can be kept in the refrigerator after cooling). Return the breasts to the pan, skin side up, and cook for 3-4 minutes to a medium-rare temperature.

■ Place the duck breast on a serving plate, place 3-4 tablespoons of the relish next to it and top with the fries.

PAN-SEARED CHICKEN BREAST WITH GRILLED TOMATILLOS SAUCE AND CORNBREAD
Serves 4

4 chicken breasts, skin removed and slightly pounded
Salt and pepper
2 tablespoons olive oil

For the Corn Bread:
1 cup ground yellow cornmeal
1 cup unbleached flour
1/3 cup sugar
2 1/2 teaspoons baking powder
1/4 teaspoon salt

1 cup soy milk
5 ounces margarine, melted and cooled
1 egg, slightly beaten
1/2 cup corn kernels
1 jalapeno pepper, seeds discarded, diced small

For the Sauce:
5 tomatillos, dry skin removed
1 jalapeno pepper

1/3 cup fresh lime juice
1 cup cilantro leaves, washed and dried
1-2 garlic cloves, sliced
Salt
1 teaspoon sugar
2 tomatoes, seeded and diced small

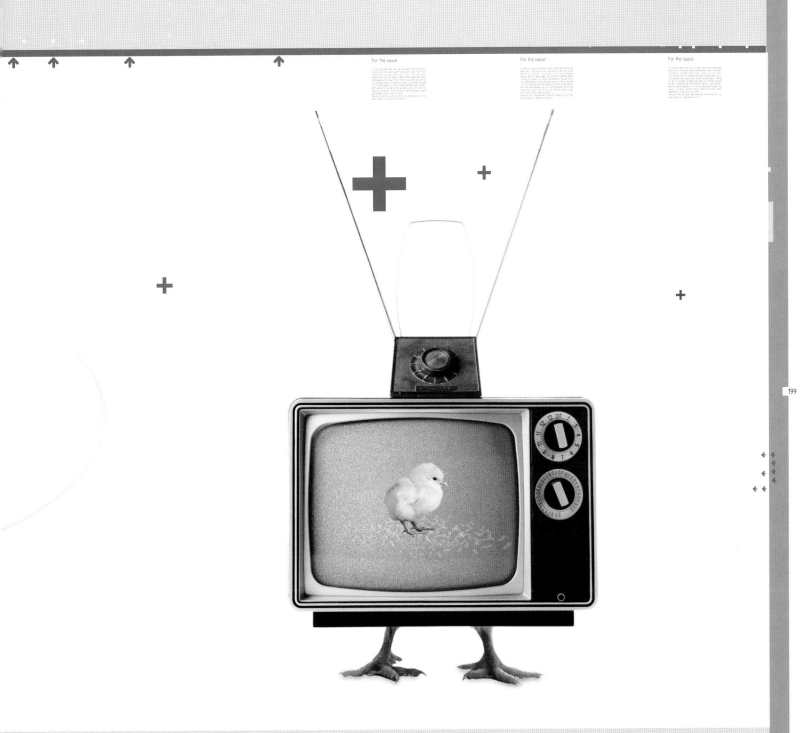

Preheat oven to 400 degrees F.

Preparation – Bread:

■ Grease a 9-inch square baking pan. In a medium size bowl mix the dry ingredients together. In another small bowl whisk the wet ingredients together. Gently mix the wet into the dry. Add the corn and jalapeno dices.

■ Pour the batter into the prepared pan and bake for 25 minutes until set and baked all the way through. Let cool before cutting into triangles.

■ In a hot grill pan, grill the tomatillos and the jalapeno pepper until soft and slightly burnt. Remove from the pan and let cool for 10 minutes. Discard the seeds from the jalapeno. In a blender, ground the tomatillos and jalapeno for 1-2 minutes. Add the cilantro leaves, lime juice, sugar and garlic. Puree for 1-2 minutes and season with salt. Keep warm

■ Season the chicken with salt and pepper. Heat the oil in a wide sauté pan and sauté the chicken breast for 4 minutes on each side, until golden and crispy. Let sit for 3 minutes and then slice each breast into 5 slices on the bias.

■ On a serving plate, fan the breast slices, drizzle the sauce around and top with two corn bread triangles. Sprinkle some of the tomato dices around and serve.

CHICKEN AND EGGPLANT ROULADES OVER VEGETABLE "SPAGHETTI" IN WARM TOMATO VINAIGRETTE

Serves 4

8 chicken cutlets (4 ounces each),
pounded 1/8- inch thick
2 medium eggplants
1/3 cup olive oil
Salt and pepper
2 cups basil leaves, washed and dried
1/2 cup pine nuts
1/3 cup extra virgin olive oil
8 slices turkey bacon
8 toothpicks

For the Vegetable "Spaghetti":

3 zucchini
3 carrots
3 yellow squash

1/2 pound green beans
3 cloves garlic
1 sprig thyme
3 tablespoons olive oil
1-2 tablespoons lemon juice

For the Vinaigrette:

2 ripe, small tomatoes
1 shallot, sliced
1 garlic clove, sliced
1/3 cup sherry vinegar
1 cup extra virgin olive oil
Pinch of sugar
Salt and pepper

eheat oven to 375 degrees F.

Slice the eggplants to 1/8-inch ck slices, lengthwise. Drizzle cup of the oil on a baking eet and place the eggplant in drizzle the other 1/4 cup of oil the eggplants and season with lt and pepper. Place in the oven 20-25 minutes (rotate in the en, if necessary). Let it cool before assembling.

■ In a blender or food processor, ground the basil leaves, pine nuts and oil for a thick smooth sauce and season with salt.

■ Brush one side of each cutlet with the pesto sauce and top with one of the eggplant slices. oll to a roulade and wrap in the ddle with a slice of the turkey con. Fasten with a toothpick. peat with the rest of the tlets and season them with lt.

With a mandolin, julienne each the vegetables and keep parate. If using a knife, cut the cchini, squash and carrots to 8-inch thick slices, lengthwise, d then cut each slice into thin long matches. Cut the green beans in quarters, lengthwise. Finely slice the

garlic. Sauté each of the vegetables with a little bit of olive oil and garlic. Season with the lemon juice, salt and pepper. Mix together in a bowl after cooking and keep warm until serving.

■ Cut the tip off the tomatoes and gently cut an X at the bottom of each. Cook the tomatoes for 30 seconds in a pot of boiling water. Remove from the water to a bowl with iced water to stop the cooking process. Peel the tomatoes, cut in half, and discard the seeds.

■ In a sauté pan, heat 1 tablespoon olive oil and sauté the garlic and sliced shallots for 1 minute. Add the tomatoes and cook for 30 seconds. Transfer to a blender or a food processor and puree for 20 seconds. Add the vinegar and sugar and drizzle the oil in while mixing. Season well with salt and pepper and keep warm.

■ In a wide sauté pan, heat the 1/3 cup of oil. Sauté the chicken roulades for 3 minutes on each side until golden. Place the "spaghetti" in the middle of a serving plate and top with 2 roulades per serving. Drizzle the outer edges with the tomato vinaigrette.

CORNMEAL CRUSTED CHICKEN SCALLOPINI OVER LEGUME HASH IN ROASTED RED PEPPER SAUCE

Serves 4

8 chicken cutlets (4 ounces each), pounded thin
2 eggs, beaten
1 cup yellow cornmeal
Salt and pepper
1/3 cup olive oil
1 red onion, diced small
2 cups fresh corn kernels (or frozen and thawed)
2 cups kidney beans, washed and drained
1 cup lima beans (if frozen, thaw before using)
4 garlic cloves, sliced
3 tablespoons Canola oil
1/3 cup chopped fresh mint leaves
Salt
1/2 teaspoon ground coriander
1/4 teaspoon cayenne pepper
1 tablespoon green tabasco sauce

For the Sauce:
2 shallots, chopped
2 garlic cloves, minced
1/4 cup olive oil
4 roasted red peppers, peeled and sliced
1 cup chicken stock
Salt and pepper
1/2 teaspoon sweet paprika
1/2 teaspoon fresh thyme leaves

1/2 cup chopped scallions (green part only) for garnish

Preparation – Sauce:

■ Heat the olive oil in a saucepan and add the shallots and garlic. Add the thyme and paprika, sauté for 1 minute, then toss in the roasted peppers. Cook for 2-3 minutes and add the vegetable stock.

Cook over high heat for 5 minutes and remove from the heat.
■ Season well with salt and pepper and check the flavors. I needed, add more paprika or garlic. Purée the sauce and strain it fo a smooth shiny texture. Keep warm.

■ In a wide sauté pan heat the oil for the legume hash. Sauté the onion and garlic for 1 minute, followed by the fresh corn kernels

and the lima beans. Sauté for 2 minutes and add the kidney beans. Season with the cayenne, coriander and salt. Check for flavor. Remove from heat and mix in the mint leaves and green tabasco (only if you serve immediately, otherwise keep the hash until serving, heat again and then season).

Mix the salt and black pepper with the cornmeal. Dredge the chicken scallopini in the beaten egg and then in the cornmeal mixture. Heat the oil in a large sauté pan and fry for 2 minutes on each side until lightly golden and crisp.

■ Place 4 tablespoons of the legume hash in the middle of a serving plate, lean 2 scallopini against it and drizzle around with sauce. Sprinkle with chopped chives.

GRILLED CHICKEN SKEWERS OVER GRILLED ZUCCHINI IN CURRY VINAIGRETTE AND CRISPY NOODLES
Serves 4

28 ounces chicken breast, boned, skinned
and cut into half-inch dices
1 pint cherry tomatoes
16 pearl onions, skinned
Salt
1/4 teaspoon cayenne pepper
Metal skewers (if using wood ones, soak
them in water for 15 minutes prior to use)

For the Vinaigrette:
1 cup + 2 tablespoons olive oil
1/2 cup chopped onions
1/2 cup chopped carrots
1/3 cup chopped celery
1/2 cup dry white wine
3 tablespoons good quality curry powder
1 tablespoon turmeric
2/3 cup chicken stock
1/2 cup white wine vinegar

3 firm green zucchini, thinly sliced
lengthwise on a mandolin or with a very
sharp knife
3 firm yellow squash, thinly sliced lengthwise
on a mandolin or with a very sharp knife
1 tablespoon thyme leaves
3 tablespoons extra virgin olive oil
Salt

1 package thin rice noodles, cooked in salted
boiling water, drained and cooled
Oil for deep-frying

Preparation – Vinaigrette:

■ Heat the 3 tablespoons oil in a sauté pan and sauté the vegetables for 3 minutes. Add the wine, curry and turmeric. Mix well and cook until the liquids are almost gone. Add the sauce and bring to a boil. Reduce to a simmer and let cook until reduced by half.

■ Strain through a fine sieve and let cool for 10 minutes.

Transfer to a bowl and drizzle the oil in, whisking constantly until the mixture starts to thicken, then alternate the oil and the vinegar for a very thick sauce. Season with salt and pepper and set aside.

■ Cook the pearl onions in boiling salted water for about 3 minutes. Drain and let cool. Alternate the chicken dices, cherry tomatoes and pearl onions on the skewers. Each serving should be 2-3 skewers. Brush with oil and season with the salt and cayenne pepper.

Heat the oil for deep-frying to 350 degrees F. Take a handful of the noodles and fry for 1-2 minutes until golden and crisp. Transfer to a plate lined with paper towel and sprinkle with salt.

Preheat oven to 350 degrees F.

Heat a grill pan or a griddle. When very hot, grill the skewers for 2-3 minutes on each side. Transfer to a baking sheet and place in the oven to finish cooking.

Brush the zucchini and squash slices with the oil and sprinkle with thyme leaves. Season with salt and pepper and grill for 30 seconds on each side.

■   On a serving plate, pile the zucchini and squash slices alternating them. Lean the skewers on top, drizzle with the curry vinaigrette and top with the fried noodles.

RED CHICKEN THIGHS IN ONION STEW WITH ZUCCHINI CAKES

Serves 4

8 chicken thighs
3 onions, sliced into 1/8-inch slices
4 garlic cloves, crushed
Salt and pepper
10 threads saffron
1/4 teaspoon ground cardamom
1/2 teaspoon ground cloves
2 tablespoons Somek (Mediterranean seasoning)
2 cups chicken or vegetable stock
1/2 cup olive oil

For the Zucchini Cakes:

2 pounds zucchini, washed, ends cut off
2 small carrots, peeled
1 tablespoon Tahini paste
1/3 cup farina
1/2 cup chopped parsley
1/3 cup chopped mint leaves
3 whole eggs
1/3 cup flour
1/2 cup breadcrumbs
1/2 cup Canola oil
1/4 cup fresh lemon juice

■ Clean the chicken thighs, season with salt and place in the refrigerator until ready to be cooked (no more than 1 hour).

■ Place the onion slices and garlic in a bottom of a dish large enough to hold all the thighs.

■ Mix all spices together and rub the thighs, thoroughly, until evenly covered. Place on top of the onions and place in the refrigerator, covered, for 2 hours.

■ Transfer the onions, garlic and thighs into a wide shallow saucepan. Add the chicken stock, bring to a boil, reduce to a simmer

and cover. Let cook for 11/2 hours until thighs are very soft and liqui[d] evaporated.

Preparation – Zucchini Cakes:

■ Grate the zucchini and carrots. Place them in a cloth and squeez[e] to get rid of excess liquids. Mix them with the farina, Tahini past[e] parsley and mint.

■ Add the eggs and combine to a consistent mixture. Season we[ll]

206

with salt and pepper and add flour slowly to achieve a thick batter (all the flour or more may be needed). Place in the refrigerator for 30 minutes to 1 hour.

■ Make patties (about 12-16) out of the mixture and roll each one in the breadcrumbs. In a wide sauté pan, heat the oil and fry the patties over medium heat 2-3 minutes on each side, until golden, crisp and firm. Remove from the pan, add the lemon juice and cook for 10 seconds. Pour over the patties. Keep warm until serving time.

Heat the oven to 500 degrees F and place an oven rack as close to the top as possible to get a broiling effect. Use a broiler if you have one.

■ Remove the thighs to an ovenproof dish. Brush them with the olive oil and broil for 4 minutes on each side.

■ Place 3 zucchini cakes on each serving plate, lean 2 thighs against them and spoon the onions around.

ROASTED GARLIC STUFFED CHICKEN BREAST OVER FENNEL CONFIT IN SAFFRON COCONUT MILK SAUCE AND BABY LEAF SALAD
Serves 4

Preheat oven to 275 degrees F.

■ With a Japanese mandolin (or a very sharp knife) slice the fennel into thin, even slices. Arrange fennel slices on a baking sheet, drizzle with oil and season with salt and pepper. Sprinkle the thyme leaves and cover with aluminum foil. Bake in the oven for 45 minutes or until the fennel is very tender but not falling apart.

■ While the fennel is baking, peel the garlic cloves, drizzl[e] with oil and wrap in foil. Place in the oven for 30 minutes o[r] until the garlic is tender. Remove from the oven.

■ Clean the chicken breast and cut it in half. With a shar[p] paring knife create a pocket in each one of them. Stuff the[m] with the roasted garlic cloves (6 each) and seal with [a] toothpick.

SAUTÉED CHICKEN LIVERS NAPOLÉON WITH PEARS IN SAFFRON HONEY SAUCE AND PUFF PASTRY

Serves 4

24 ounces chicken livers, very fresh and cleaned

2 tablespoons Dramboui

Salt and pepper

2 tablespoons duck fat or margarine

1 package frozen puff pastry, or wonton raps

4 big Bosc pears, peeled, cored and each cut into 6 slices

(lengthwise)

1/2 cup wild flower honey

1/4 cup water

Juice from 1 lemon

10 threads saffron

1/2 teaspoon black pepper

■ Mix the chicken livers with the Dramboui, cover and place in the refrigerator until ready to be cooked.

Preheat oven to 425 degrees F.

■ Place the puff pastry on a lightly floured surface. With a sharp knife, cut each sheet into 3 x 3-inch squares. There should be eight.

■ Line a baking sheet with parchment paper, transfer the puff pastry onto the sheet and cover with another parchment paper and another baking sheet. The aim is to bake the pastry without puffing a lot. Bake for about 20 minutes until light brown on the top as well as the bottom. Remove the top baking sheet and parchment and let cool.

■ Mix the pear slices with the lemon juice. In a wide saucepot, mix the honey and the water and bring to a boil while stirring. Add the pears and black pepper to the liquids and cook over low heat for 15-20 minutes. Remove the pears, add the saffron to the sauce and cook for 2 more minutes. Keep warm until ready to be served.

■ Heat the duck fat in a wide sauté pan. Strain the livers, season with salt and pepper and sauté them for 2 minutes on each side. Do not overcrowd the pan (do it in 2 batches, if needed). The livers are done when they are still pink inside but brown outside.

■ On a serving plate, place half of a serving portion of the livers in the middle. Top with one pastry square, place the other half of the livers and top with another pastry. Surround with pears and drizzle with the sauce. Serve immediately.

STIR-FRIED CHICKEN IN PEANUT SAUCE OVER RICE NOODLES AND SAUTÉED SNOW PEAS

Serves 4

4 chicken breasts (about 7ounces each), boned and
skinned, sliced into 1/8-inch slices
Salt and pepper
1 tablespoon chopped fresh ginger
1 red pepper, seeds removed, sliced

For the Sauce:

5 ounces roasted peanuts
2 tablespoons peanut oil
1 medium onion, chopped
1 teaspoon red pepper flakes
4 garlic cloves, minced
1 tablespoon dark brown sugar
3 Kefir lime leaves
1 tablespoon fresh lemon juice
1/2 teaspoon ground coriander
2 cups chicken stock
1/3 cup coconut milk
1/2 cup sweet soy sauce

1 pound snow peas, growing tip cut off
3 garlic cloves, chopped
2 tablespoons peanut oil

1 pound wide rice noodles, cooked
2 tablespoons peanut oil
1/2 tablespoon turmeric powder

1/2 cup chopped roasted peanuts for garnish

Preparation — Sauce:

■ Ground the peanuts in a food processor to a smooth texture. In a sauté pan, heat the oil and sauté the onion and garlic for 1 minute. Add the pepper flakes, sugar, lime leaves and coriander and cook for one minute. Add the peanut paste, mix well and reduce to a low heat. Add the stock gradually while stirring until you get a thick rich texture. Add the sweet soy sauce, coconut milk and remove from the heat.

■ Bring water to boil in a pot, add salt and cook snow peas for 2 minutes. Drain and transfer the snow peas to a bowl with ice water to stop the cooking. Drain.

■ In a wok, or a wide sauté pan, heat the oil for the snow peas. Add the garlic and cook for 20 seconds until golden. Add the snow peas and sauté for 1 minute. Season with salt and pepper and set aside.

■ Using the same wok, heat the oil for the chicken. Season the chicken slices with salt and pepper and sauté for 1 minute. Add the ginger and peppers and stir-fry for 2 more minutes. Remove from the wok to a warm place.

■ Add the oil for the noodles to the wok, sprinkle with the turmeric and add the noodles. Sauté for 30 seconds and add the snow peas. Turn off the heat and remove from the wok to serving bowls. Top the noodles with the chicken and drizzle with the peanut sauce. Sprinkle with the chopped peanuts.

BRAISED DUCK LEGS OVER LENTIL RAGOUT AND ROASTED BABY BOK CHOY

Serves 4

8 duck legs
1/2 cup duck fat or chicken fat
1 onion, halved and sliced
1 carrot, thinly sliced
3 cups red wine
2 cups chicken stock
3 sprigs Italian parsley
2 bay leaves

2 sprigs fresh thyme
16 baby carrots, peeled
12 baby white turnips, peeled, tops saved for later
1 cup white pearl onions, blanched and skinned

For the Lentils:

2 cups French lentils
1/2 cup diced onion

Preheat oven to 400 degrees F.

Brush the duck legs with duck fat and brown well in the oven (about 40 minutes). In a wide braising pot sauté the onion and carrot in olive oil or duck fat. Get rid of excess fat and add wine. Reduce by half. Add chicken broth, parsley, bay leaves, thyme, and the well-browned duck legs. Cover tightly and return to oven, reduced to 325 degrees F. Braise for about 1 hour.

Preparation — Ragout:

■ In a wide saucepot, heat the oil and sauté the onion, carrots, celery and garlic for 2 minutes. Add the lentils, wine and stock. Bring to a boil and reduce to a simmer. Add the thyme leaves and season with salt. Cook, covered, for about 20 minutes until all liquids are gone. Add the cream and cook for 5 additional minutes. The lentils should be soft. Keep warm.

■ Rub the baby bok choy with the oil and season with salt and pepper. Place in a baking sheet, cover with foil and bake for 15 minutes. Remove foil and bake 10 additional minutes. Remove from the oven and keep warm.

■ Meanwhile, bring water to a boil in a medium pot and salt well. Cook the carrots and turnips and onions for 3-4 minutes and drain.

■ When the duck legs are cooked, transfer them to a platter. Strain the sauce into a glass bowl and separate the fat from the juice (the fat will float).

■ Heat the vegetables in the defatted sauce for a few minutes. Pour sauce over duck legs. Place 3-4 tablespoons of the lentil ragout in the middle of a serving plate, cross 2 duck legs over the ragout and top with sauce. Spread some of the baby vegetables around the legs and fan the baby bok choy.

1/2 cup peeled and diced carrot
1/2 cup diced celery
2 tablespoons olive oil
4 garlic cloves, minced
2 cups chicken stock
1 cup red wine
Salt
1 tablespoon fresh thyme leaves

PAN-SEARED DUCK BREAST WITH BERRY SAUCE, CORN CUSTARD AND FRISEE SALAD

Serves 4

4 duck breasts, about 8 ounces each, unskinned	1/2 cup corn meal	2 shallots, chopped
	Pinch of sugar	1 tablespoon Canola oil
Salt and pepper	Pinch all spice	1 cup blackberries
	1/2 teaspoon cayenne	2 cups blueberries
For the Custard:	1 teaspoon salt	2 cups port wine
	1/2 teaspoon pepper	11/2 cups chicken stock
3 cups corn kernels	1/4 cup chopped parsley leaves	1 sprig tarragon
2 cups non-dairy heavy cream	1/4 cup chopped basil leaves	Pinch of ground cardamom
3 large eggs	Vegetable oil spray	1/4 teaspoon salt

Preheat oven to 325 degrees F.

Prepare the Custard:

■   Oil soufflé dishes with the oil spray. In a large bowl, mix the cream and the eggs. Add the cornmeal, whisking well to avoid lumps. Add the seasonings and fresh herbs and mix. Add the corn kernels. Pour the batter into the baking dishes 3/4 full. Place the dishes in a deep baking sheet and fill the sheet with water. The water should cover half the height of the soufflé dishes. Bake for about 45 minutes until the custard is set in the middle. Let cool and then gently, using a knife to allow for easy remoal, flip each custard, upside down, on to the middle of a serving plate (1 per person).

■   While the custard is baking prepare the sauce (sauce can be done ahead of time as well). In a wide saucepot heat the oil, sauté the shallots for 1 minute, add the wine and the stock and bring to a boil.

MADE IN BROOKLYN, NEW YORK, USA

1 head frisse lettuce, core removed
and leaves washed and dried
2 tablespoons sherry wine vinegar
4 tablespoons extra virgin olive oil
Salt

■ Add the tarragon, cardamom and salt and reduce by half. Add the berries and cook for 10 minutes. Check for flavor. If too acidic add 1 tablespoon honey. Strain the sauce through a fine strainer and bring to a boil in a pot. The sauce should be thick and dark in color.

■ Score the duck fat (skin) with a sharp knife. Heat a heavy pan and place the duck, skin side down to render the fat, about 10 minutes over medium heat. Remove the breasts, season them with salt and pepper and get rid of the excess fat (can be kept in the refrigerator).

■ Return the breasts to the pan, skin side up and cook for 3-4 minutes to a medium rare temperature. Let sit for 3-4 minutes and then cut to 1/4-inch slices on the bias.

■ Mix the frisee with the vinegar and oil, season with salt.

■ Fan the duck slices around the custard, like a flower. Drizzle the sauce on top of the duck and top the custard with the frisee salad. Serve.

GRILLED DUCK BREAST OVER CRISPY DICED POTATOES WITH MUSHROOM STEW

Serves 4

For the sauce:

In a big pot warm the olive oil and sweat the onions and garlic until the onions are translucent. Add the diced butternut squash and sauf for 3-4 minutes. Season with salt and pepper and add the vegetable stock. The liquids should just cover the butternut squash. Bring to a boil and reduce to medium-low heat. Let simmer covered for 35-40 minutes until the butternut squash is very tender. With emulsifier blender (or in a food processor) Puree the sauce to an even, smooth texture. Add the heavy cream and bring to a boil over low heat. Remove from the heat basil leaves

For the sauce:

In a big pot warm the olive oil and sweat the onions and garlic until the onions are translucent. Add the diced butternut squash and sauf for 3-4 minutes. Season with salt and pepper and add the vegetable stock. The liquids should just cover the butternut squash. Bring to a boil and reduce to medium-low heat. Let simmer covered for 35-40 minutes until the butternut squash is very tender. With emulsifier blender (or in a food processor) Puree the sauce to an even, smooth texture. Add the heavy cream and bring to a boil over low heat. Remove from the heat and taste for seasoning. Cut the basil leaves into juliennes and mix in.

4 duck breasts, 7 ounces each, skin removed and sliced1/8-inch thick, on the bias	5 ounces Shiitake mushrooms, stem removed, sliced	3 tablespoons olive oil
Salt and pepper	5 ounces Cremini mushrooms, sliced	2 tablespoons good brandy or cognac
1 tablespoon olive oil	3 ounces Black Trumpet mushrooms (if sandy, wash gently)	1 sprig thyme
1 Vidalia onion (or other sweet onion), halved and thinly sliced	3 ounce dried Porcini mushrooms or 5 ounces fresh ones	2 sprigs tarragon
4-5 Yukon gold potatoes, peeled and diced (1/4 inch)	4 ounce Chanterelle mushrooms	2 sprigs parsley
1/4 cup olive oil	4 garlic cloves, lightly crushed	1/2 teaspoon fennel seeds
Salt and pepper	2 shallots, thinly sliced	2 bay leaves
5 ounces Button mushrooms, sliced	1 1/2 cups dark beef stock or chicken stock	Cheesecloth
		Twine
		Sea salt and pepper
		1/3 cup chopped fresh basil leaves
		Truffle oil

■ Place the potato dices in a pot and cover with cold water. Add salt. Bring the water to a boil. Drain and transfer the potatoes into a bowl with ice water to stop the cooking. Drain again and let sit for 5 minutes to get rid of excess water.

■ If using dried mushrooms, soak them in hot water (water should cover the mushrooms) for 7 minutes. Drain but keep the water aside.

Preparation – Stew:

■ With a short, sharp knife, cut the tip of the stem of the Chanterelle mushrooms and gently peel the outside layer of the stems. If large, cut them into quarters. Place all herbs and seasonings in the cheesecloth and tie with a twine. Heat the olive oil in a wide saucepot and sauté the shallot slices and garlic for 1 minute. Add the brandy, tilting the pan away from you to avoid a flame if flambé. Add the Shiitake, Cremini and Button mushrooms and sauté while stirring for 1 minute. Add the dried Porcini and the Chanterelle and season well with salt and pepper. Add the stock, 1/2 cup from the dried

mushroom liquids and the herbs and cook, uncovered, over a low-medium flame, for 30 minutes. Immediately before serving mix in the basil leaves.

Preparation – Potatoes:

■ Heat 1 tablespoon of the oil in a wide sauté pan (preferably a non-stick one) and sauté the onions until golden brown, about 5-7 minutes. Remove from the pan and set aside. Heat the rest of the oil until very hot and add the potatoes. Sauté them, mixing occasionally, until golden and crisp. Add the onions to the potatoes and sauté for 1 minute. Season well with salt and pepper and place in the middle of a serving plate.

■ Brush the duck slices with the oil and season with salt and pepper. Heat a grill pan or a griddle and when very hot grill the duck slices 30 seconds on each side. Fan the slices against the potatoes and spoon the mushroom stew around. Drizzle a few drops of the truffle oil on top of the duck (it is very strong in flavor) and serve.

BRAISED TURKEY BREAST WITH TAPANADE STUFFING OVER VEGETABLE RATATOUILLE
Serves 4

- 1 turkey breast, about 2 pounds ■ Salt and pepper ■ 3 toothpicks ■ 1/3 cup Canola oil nuts ■ 1 teaspoon cider vinegar ■ 1 onion, sliced ■ 1 eggplant, diced ■ 2 zucchini, dice ■ 3 tablespoons olive oil ■ 1 teaspoon fresh thyme leaves ■ 1/2 cup chopped parsley

Preparation – Tapanade:

■ Place the olives, anchovies and vinegar in a food processor. Puree for 1 minute and add the garlic and pine nuts. Puree until the garlic is chopped. Season with salt and puree again for 30 seconds.

■ Using a very sharp knife, make a pocket in the turkey breast, inserting the knife from the breast's side and toward the inner right side of the breast (moving your hand toward the left so the pocket's opening will be about 2 inches wide).

Preheat oven to 375 degrees F.

■ Spread the tapanade paste with your hand or using an offset spatula in the pocket and seal with the toothpicks. Season the turkey with salt and pepper.

■ Heat the oil in a wide sauté pan and sear the turkey for 4- minutes on each side. Transfer to a deep baking dish, pour the stoc on the bottom and sprinkle with the orange zest.

■ Place in the oven and braise for 40-45 minute flipping the breast at least once to prevent the to from drying out. Remove from the oven and let si for 10 minutes before slicing. Transfer the liquids to a pan and let simmer for 15 minutes Use as the sauce.

■ While the turkey is in the oven, prepar the ratatouille: Heat skillet and add oliv oil to coat pan. Sauté onions in oil unt soft. Add garlic and sauté until soft. Ad the eggplant, cook for 1 minute and ad the red pepper, the rest of the vegetables, and season with salt, peppe and thyme. Garnish with minced parsley

■ Slice the stuffed turkey breast (2 slice per person). Spread the ratatouille on serving plate and place the turkey slice overlapping in the middle. Mix the greens wit the oil, lemon juice and za'atar, season with sa and pile on the turkey slices. Drizzle some of the sauce from the turkey and serve.

2 cups chicken stock ■ Zest from 1 orange ■ 4 cups black olives, pitted ■ 4 anchovy fillets ■ 2 garlic cloves ■ 1/2 cup pine
2 yellow squash, diced ■ 1 red pepper, diced ■ 3 tomatoes, diced ■ 1 clove garlic, minced ■ Salt and pepper
■ 2 cups salad greens ■ 2 tablespoons extra virgin olive oil ■ 1 tablespoon fresh lemon juice ■ 1 teaspoon Za'atar

BUTTERNUT SQUASH BOATS WITH TURKEY STUFFING, SAUTÉED SWISS CHARD "LASAGNA" IN CHICKEN REDUCTION SAUCE

Serves 4

Preheat oven to 350 degrees F.

■ Cut the squash in half, lengthwise, and use a spoon to discard the seeds.

■ In a sauté pan, heat the chicken fat until clear and sauté the garlic and

onion for 1 minute until onion is translucent. Keep the pan aside to cool.

■ Mix the turkey meat with the seasoning in a mixing bowl. In a separate bowl, mix the cream with the eggs. Add the onion, garlic and fat to the meat. Combine well and add the egg mixture. Stir just until combined. To taste for flavor, cook a small portion of the meat and season accordingly.

■ Stuff the middle of the halved squash (where the seeds were) with the stuffing and place in a deep baking dish. Sprinkle with salt and pepper and pour 2 cups of the chicken stock into the pan. Add the sage and cover with foil. Bake for 45 minutes then

remove foil and bake for 15-20 additional minutes. Remove from the oven. Add the liquids from the pan to the reduction sauce.

Preparation — Sauce:

Heat the oil in a saucepot and sauté the vegetables for 3- minutes. Add the stock and scorch the bottom of the pot. Bring to a boil and reduce to a simmer. Place all the aromatics in the cheesecloth and tie well. Place the cloth in the pot, let simmer and reduce by 2/3 until the sauce golden brown (about 40 minutes).

■ Meanwhile, bring a pot with water to boil. Salt the water and cook the lasagna leaves dente (fresh pasta, about 2- minutes; dry pasta about 8-10 Drain and toss with a little olive oil avoid sticking. Spread on a tray.

■ In a wide sauté pan, heat the 1/2 of the oil for the Swiss chard Add 1/2 of the garlic and sauté the green Swiss chard for minute. Season with salt and pepper and remove from the pan to a strainer to get rid of excess liquids. Repeat with the re Swiss chard.

■ On a serving plate, alternate the lasagna leaves with the re and green chard to create "free form lasagna." Cut each boat i half, lengthwise (optional), careful not to take the stuffing ou and lean against the lasagna. Spoon the sauce around an sprinkle with tarragon leaves.

2 medium butternut squash

11/2 pounds ground turkey meat

3 tablespoons chicken or duck fat

1 medium onion, diced small

2 garlic cloves, minced

2 eggs + 1 yolk

1/3 cup non-dairy heavy cream

1/2 teaspoon ground mustard seeds

Pinch of nutmeg

Pinch chili pepper

1 sprig sage

1 bunch green chard, washed, white part removed

1 bunch red Swiss chard, washed, white part removed

1 pound fresh lasagna leaves or 1 package lasagna leaves

3 tablespoons olive oil

2 garlic cloves, chopped

Salt and pepper

11/2 quarts chicken stock at room temperature

1/2 cup diced onion

1/2 cup peeled and diced carrot

1/2 cup diced celery

Cheesecloth

2 sprigs thyme

2 sprigs tarragon

2 sprigs parsley

1 bay leaf

2 tablespoons Canola oil

1/3 cup fresh tarragon leaves

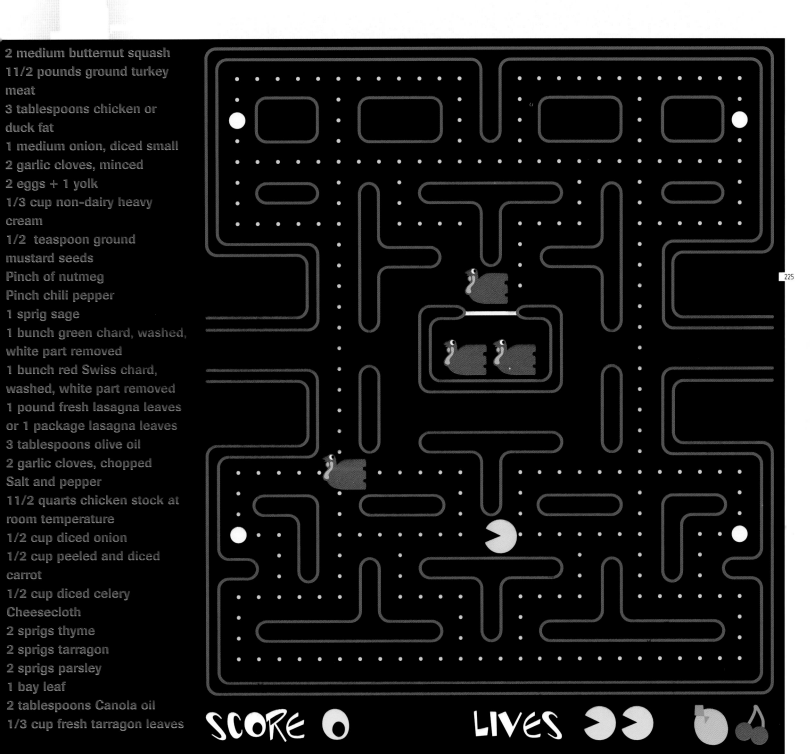

OVEN-ROASTED CORNISH HENS WITH DATES AND GARLIC STUFFING OVER WILD RICE IN WHITE WINE SAUCE

Serves 4

2 Cornish hens, about 11/2-2 pounds each
Salt and pepper
1/3 cup chopped rosemary leaves

2 cups moist dates, chopped
5 Challa bread slices, crust removed
10 garlic cloves
2 tablespoons extra virgin olive oil
3 shallots, chopped
1/2 cup sherry or Marsala wine

1 cup chopped parsley
1/2 teaspoon cumin
1/4 teaspoon cinnamon
1/4 teaspoon ground cloves
1/4 teaspoon chili powder
Salt

For the Sauce:
2 tablespoons olive oil
1 cup diced onion

1 cup diced carrots
1/2 cup diced celery
2 sprigs thyme
1 sprig sage
1 bottle semi-dry white wine

2 cups wild rice
3 cups chicken stock
1 tablespoon olive oil
Salt and pepper

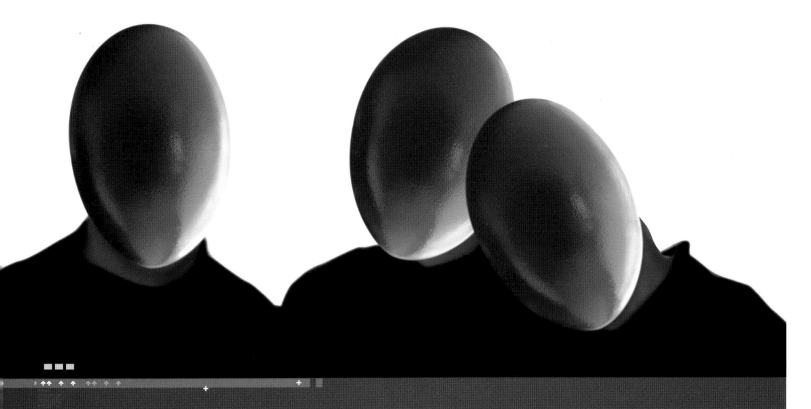

Preheat oven to 400 degrees F.

Preparation — Stuffing:

■ Cut the bread into quarter-inch dices and toast in the oven. Place the garlic cloves in aluminum foil, drizzle with the oil, seal the foil and roast for 15-20 minutes until cloves are golden and soft.

■ Mix all the stuffing ingredients in a big bowl. Check for flavor and season accordingly. Season the cavity of the hens with salt and pepper and stuff it with the stuffing.

■ Truss chicken, brush with olive oil and season with salt, pepper and rosemary. Place chicken in a roasting pan and roast at 400 degrees F for 30 minutes. Baste chicken with olive oil and turn roast. Reduce the temperature to 350 degrees F for another half hour or until internal temperature is 180 and juices run clear. Remove from the roasting pan and allow to rest for 10 minutes before cutting. While the hens roast prepare the sauce and cook the rice.

Preparation — Sauce:

■ In a wide saucepan, heat the oil and sauté the vegetables for 3 minutes. Add the wine and herbs, bring to a boil and reduce to a simmer. Let cook until reduced by two thirds. When the hens are ready, add the liquids from the roasting pan to the sauce and cook for 5 minutes. Strain and keep warm until serving time.

■ Heat the oil for the rice in a pot, sauté the rice for 20 seconds and add the stock. Season with salt and pepper, bring to a boil and reduce to a low flame. Cover the pot and let cook for about 40 minutes, making sure there are enough liquids. The rice grains should be tender and split a little.

■ Cut each chicken in half (lengthwise) and then each half into a leg and breast part. Pile some of the rice in the middle of a serving plate, lean the breast and leg against it and spoon the sauce on top and around. Serve.

GRILLED QUAIL WITH BALSAMIC AND HONEY OVER SPINACH RISOTTO AND BRAISED LEEKS

Serves 4

■ Mix the balsamic vinegar with the honey and thyme sprigs. Rub the quails well with salt and pepper and place them in the marinade. Transfer to a dish that will fit all and let marinate in the refrigerator for at least 2 hours (up to 12 hours).

Preheat oven to 375 degrees F.

■ Place the leeks in a baking pan. Mix the wine and stock in a small bowl and pour over the leeks. Season with salt and pepper and cover with aluminum foil. Braise in the oven for 30 minutes. Remove foil and braise for 15-20 additional minutes until leeks are very soft and golden. Keep the liquids.

Preparation – Risotto:

■ Heat the margarine in a wide sauté pan until melted. Add the spinach leaves and season with salt and pepper. Cook over medium high flame until spinach is soft and dark green.

■ Remove from the pan and spread on a baking sheet for faster cooling. When cool, ground the spinach to a dark green, smooth texture in a blender or a food processor.

■ In a big wide pot, heat the oil and sauté the onions and garlic for 2 minutes. Add the rice and the white wine, mixing constantly. When liquids evaporate, add one cup of the chicken stock at a time. Continue mixing until liquids evaporate. Continue until rice is fully cooked about 18-20 minutes. Add the spinach puree and cream. Season well with salt and pepper and cook for 5 additional minutes. Remove from the heat but keep warm.

■ Heat a griddle or a wide grill pan. Remove the quails from the marinade and pat dry. Brush them with olive oil and grill, skin side down, for 5 minutes. Turn over and grill for 3 additional minutes. Cut in half.

■ Put 5 tablespoons of the risotto in a middle of a serving plate, cross the two halves against the risotto and top with two leeks. Drizzle around with some of the leek braising liquids and serve.

■ 4 quails or squabs, about 1 pound each, backbone and breastbone removed ■ 1 bottle good balsamic vinegar ■ 2/3 cup well washed ■ 1/2 cup chicken stock ■ 2/3 cups semi sweet white wine ■ 1 small onion, diced ■ 2 garlic cloves, minced ■ 1 1/2 quarts chicken stock ■ 1/3 cup non-dairy cream ■ 3 cups spinach leaves, washed and dried ■ 1 tablespoon margarine

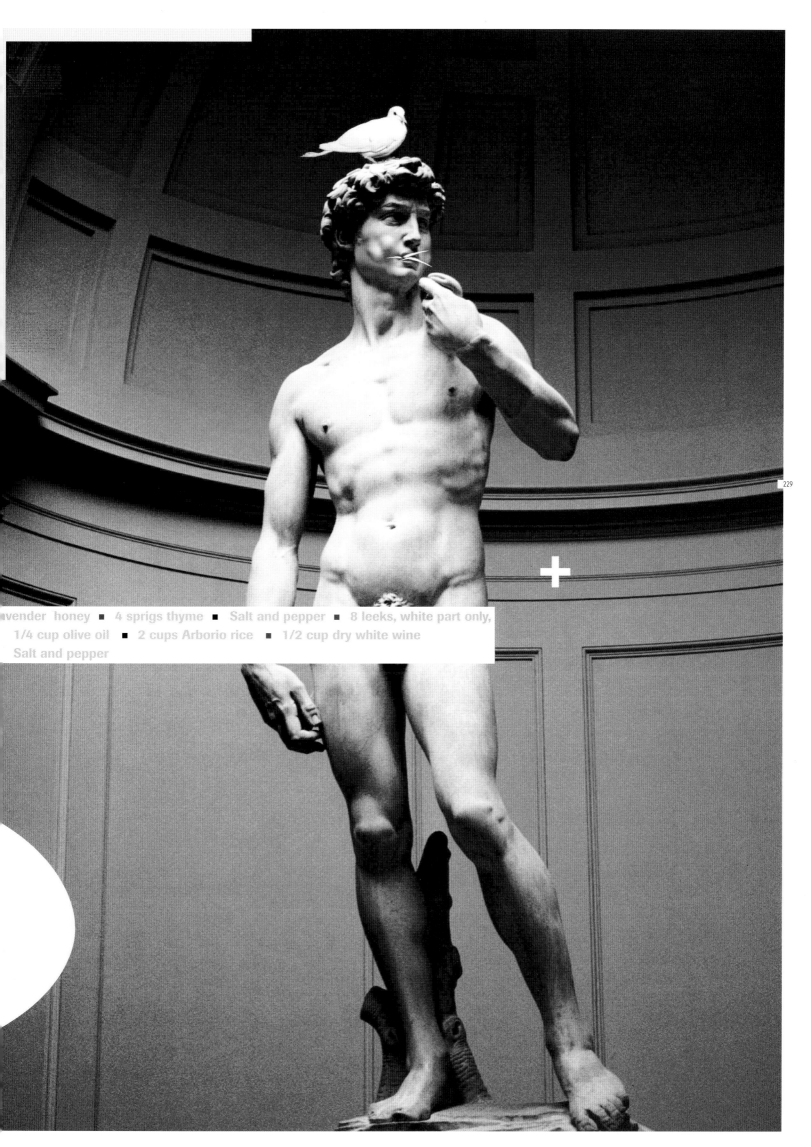

vender honey ■ 4 sprigs thyme ■ Salt and pepper ■ 8 leeks, white part only,
1/4 cup olive oil ■ 2 cups Arborio rice ■ 1/2 cup dry white wine
Salt and pepper

FOOD EMBRACES ELEMENTS FROM OUR PAST. IT IS A PART OF OUR HISTORY AS A BEING, A FAMILY OR A NATION. IT IS FUNDAMENTAL IN CREATING CHERISHED MEMORIES.

MEAT

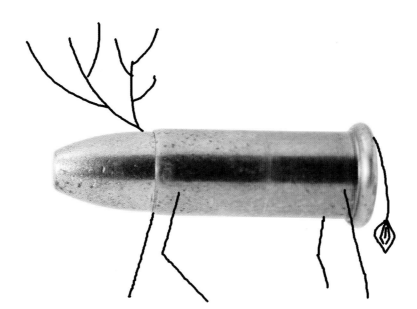

SHELL STEAK WITH COLD RICE SALAD AND CHIMICHURRI SAUCE

Serves 4

4 8-ounce shell steaks
1 1/2 cups cilantro
1 cup parsley
3 fresh bay leaves
2 teaspoons ground cumin
1/4 cup fresh oregano leaves
1/4 cup fresh thyme leaves
2 teaspoons ground pepper
1 tablespoon salt

1 cup chopped onion
1/2 cup chopped garlic
1 1/3 cup distilled vinegar
1/2 cup Canola oil
1/3 cup olive oil
1 jalapeno pepper, seeds removed, chopped

2 cups Basmati rice
3 cups water
2 tablespoons Turmeric powder
1 tablespoon salt
2 medium onions, halved and sliced
4 tablespoons olive oil
1 cup currants
1 1/2 cups warm water

Preparation – Sauce:

■ Place the cumin, herbs, onion and garlic in a blender. When well chipped add the vinegar and slowly add the oil. Season well with salt and pepper.

■ Divide into two batches. Add the jalapeno pepper to one part and keep in the refrigerator for later use (this is the sauce).

■ Place the other part in a bowl, add steak and marinate. Cover for 2 hours and refrigerate.

Preparation – Rice

■ In a mixing bowl, cover the currants with the warm water and soak for 15 minutes. Strain and set aside. Heat 2 tablespoons oil in a pot, add the rice and mix for 10 seconds.

Add the turmeric powder and mix. Add the water and salt and bring to a boil. Once boiling, reduce to a low heat and cover the pot. Cook, undisturbed, for 20 minutes or until the rice is tender and all the water is gone. Remove the lid and let steam for 5 minutes then transfer to a big mixing bowl.

While the rice is cooking heat the remaining 2 tablespoons of oil in a sauté pan and add the onion slices, stirring well. Reduce to a medium heat and continue cooking until the onion is tender and golden.

Mix the rice with the onion and the currants and season with salt and pepper. Let cool (can be served warm or cold).

Dry steaks and grill on a hot grilling pan or a griddle for 3 minutes per side. Season with salt and slice.

On a serving plate, arrange the cold rice salad and surround with steak slices. Drizzle with the Chimichurri sauce and serve.

ORANGE AND COGNAC BEEF STEW OVER EGG NOODLES
Serves 4

3 pounds hangar steak, trimmed and cut into 1-inch cubes
1/2 cup flour
4 tablespoons Canola oil
2 onions, thinly sliced
2 cloves garlic, smashed and minced
1 pound Cremini mushrooms, quartered
1 cup red wine (Merlot or Cabernet)
4 tablespoons tomato paste
4 carrots, peeled and sliced into 1/4-inch rounds
1 sprig fresh rosemary
1 sprig fresh sage
2 sprigs fresh thyme
1/4 cup good quality cognac or brandy
Juice of 1 orange, plus 2 strips of zest
Olive oil
Salt and pepper
1 pound flat egg noodles
3 tablespoons extra virgin olive oil
1/2 cup chopped chives
16 orange fillets for garnish (unsweetened mandarin oranges or fresh)

■ Season steak with salt and pepper and toss with the flour. Get rid of the excess flour. In a large, deep, heavy pot, heat Canola oil. Add meat to the pot to brown lightly. Do not crowd the pot – brown in batches, if necessary. When steak is browned on all sides, remove from pot.

■   Add onions, garlic and mushrooms and stir well. Use a wooden spoon to scratch bottom. Add red wine, stirring until wine reduces by half.

■   Return meat to the pot; add tomato paste, carrots and herbs. Cover with 2 inches of water, add cognac and orange zest and simmer, covered partially, for 1-2 hours, until steak is tender.

■ Remove herb stems and zest pieces from pot. Add orange juice and simmer 15 minutes more.

■ Cook the noodles in boiling salted water for about 8 minutes. Drain and toss with the oil and chopped chives, season with salt. Serve the stew over the noodles and garnish with orange fillets.

HERBS AND GARLIC ROASTED LOIN OF LAMB WITH ROASTED FINGERLING POTATOES
Serves 6

Preheat oven to 450 degrees F.

■ Make a mixture with 1/2 cup olive oil, Dijon and whole sprigs of herbs and garlic. Marinate the lamb for at least one hour. Place lamb in a heavy ovenproof casserole dish that will hold lamb comfortably. Place cut vegetables around base of pan. Season generously with salt and pepper. Turn oven down to 400 degrees F. Bake for 40 minutes, rotating lamb.

When finished, an instant thermometer reading inserted in the center should register 120 degrees for medium rare.

Preparation – Potatoes

■ Mix potatoes with the rosemary, oil and salt and place in a baking sheet and cover with aluminum

loin of lamb, approximately 4 pounds

3/4 cup extra virgin olive oil

1/2 cup Dijon mustard

large cloves garlic, smashed

sprigs thyme

sprigs rosemary

cup diced onion

1/2 cup diced celery stalks

1/2 cup diced carrots

1 leek (white part only) washed and sliced to 1/8 inch

1 cup red wine (Merlot or Cabernet)

11/2 pounds fingerling potatoes

1/4 cup olive oil

2 tablespoons fresh rosemary leaves

Salt and pepper

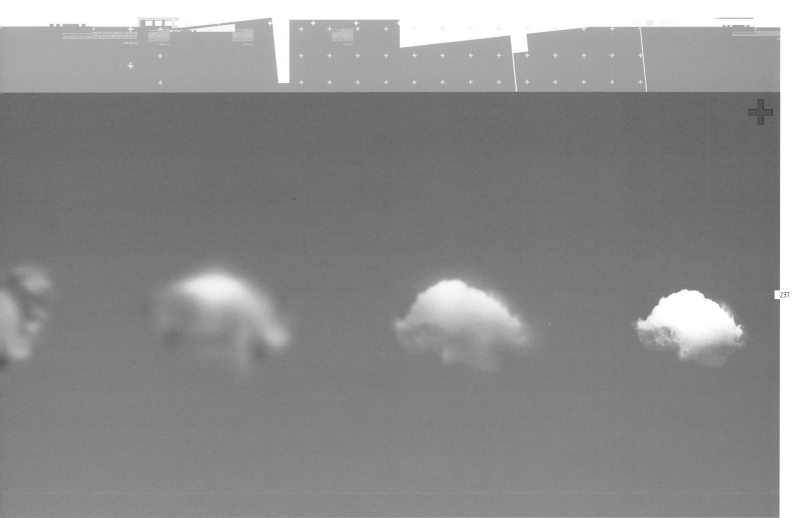

foil. Roast in the oven for 30 minutes then remove foil and roast for 15 additional minutes until lightly golden and crisp. Remove from the oven and keep warm until ready to be served.

■ Remove lamb from oven and place in a shallow baking pan tented with foil, set aside 15 minutes before slicing. Slice 1/2 inch thick, on the bias (3-4 slices per person).

■ Transfer contents of casserole into saucepan. Add the wine to the casserole and scratch the bottom with a wooden spoon (the wine should boil immediately). Bring contents of saucepan to a simmer. Peel remaining garlic and add remainder of herb sprigs. Simmer gently for 30 minutes. Strain, return to saucepan and season with salt and pepper. Serve the lamb over the roasted potatoes and drizzle with the sauce.

BRAISED LAMB CHOPS IN LEMON SAUCE WITH CORN AND GRAIN CAKES

Serves 4

8 lamb chops (not trimmed) at room temperature
1/4 cup olive oil
Salt and pepper
2 garlic cloves, peeled
2 shallots, peeled and chopped
1/4 cup flour
1 egg, beaten
Juice from 1 large lemon
2 cups beef or lamb stock
1/3 cup chopped mint leaves for garnish
1 lemon, quartered

4 1/2 ounces quinoa
3 ounces corn (canned or frozen and thawed)
1 1/2 quarts vegetable stock
1 teaspoon salt
Ground black pepper (as needed)
12 ounces yellow cornmeal
3/4 teaspoon ground cumin
1/2 teaspoon cayenne
4 1/2 ounces cornflake crumbs
1/2 teaspoon vegetable oil

■ Season the chops with salt and pepper, coat in the flour and then in the egg. Heat the oil in a big sauté pan and sauté the chops until golden on both sides. Remove from the pan to a big wide brazing pot that will fit all chops in one layer. In the sauté pan sauté the potatoes, in batches, in the remaining fat for 5 minutes until lightly golden and crisp.

■ Mix the lemon juice with the stock, garlic and shallots and pour over the chops. Season with salt and pepper. Bring to a boil and reduce to low heat. Cook, covered for 1 1/2 hours. Add more liquids if necessary.

Preparation – Cakes:

■ Rinse the quinoa several times in cold water and drain.

■ Cook the quinoa in two cups of the stock, about 15 minutes. Fluff with a fork and spread on a sheet pan to cool. Season with 1/4 teaspoon salt and pepper.

Bring the remaining 1 quart of stock to a boil. Whisking constantly, gradually add 6 ounces of the cornmeal to the stock. Reduce to a simmer and continue to cook for 30 minutes, stirring constantly.

Remove from the heat and stir in the corn, quinoa, cumin and cayenne. Season with 1/2 teaspoon salt and taste for flavor. Correct seasoning as needed. Pour into half sheet pan to cool.

When cool enough to handle, form the mixture into 20 cakes, about 2 1/2 ounces each. Refrigerate until needed.

■ Combine the remaining cornmeal with the cornflake crumbs. Heat the oil in a sauté pan; dredge the cakes in the cornmeal mixture and fry for 2 minutes on each side.

■ Place two cakes in each serving plate, lean 2 chops against the cakes and drizzle with the sauce. Garnish with the mint leaves and lemon quarters.

HERB CRUSTED RACK OF LAMB WITH ROASTED PUMPKIN RAVIOLI IN LIGHT VINAIGRETTE
Serves 4

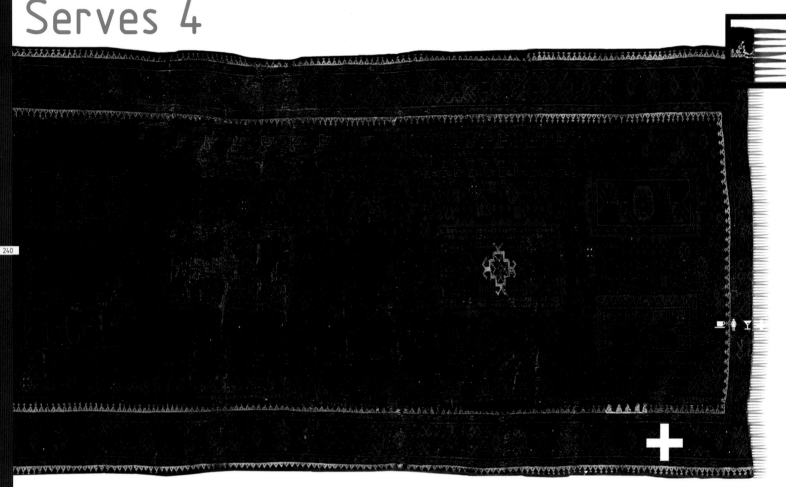

3 tablespoons canola oil

2 racks of lamb, cleaned and frenched

6 slices good quality stale white bread

2 tablespoons chopped fresh mint

2 tablespoons chopped fresh parsley

2 tablespoons chopped fresh chives

2 tablespoons chopped fresh basil

1 tablespoon extra virgin olive oil

2 tablespoons grainy Dijon mustard

1 pack round Wonton/Gyoza skins

Preheat oven to 400 degrees F.

Preparation — Vinaigrette:

■ In a mixing bowl mix the lemon juice, chopped shallot, garlic and mustard with a whisk. While whisking add the oil slowly to create emulsification. Season with salt and pepper and check the flavors. If the vinaigrette is too tart add a little more oil, and if too "oily" add more lemon juice and mustard.

Preparation — Ravioli:

■ Cut the pumpkin into 2 x 2 inch pieces. Brush each piece with olive oil, season with salt and pepper and sprinkle lightly with the sugar (or honey). Arrange on a baking sheet and cover with foil. Place the garlic cloves on a separate piece of foil and seal it.

■ Bake the pumpkin and garlic in the oven for 20 minutes, remove garlic (make sure it's tender) and then remove foil from the squash and bake for an additional 15 minutes until pieces are tender and golden. Let cool for 10-15 minutes.

2 egg whites
1 pound pumpkin, peeled
1/2 cup olive oil
2 tablespoons brown sugar or honey
7-8 garlic cloves
1/2 cup lemon juice

1 tablespoon chopped shallot
1 small garlic clove, minced
1 teaspoon Dijon mustard
1 cup extra virgin olive oil
Salt and black pepper

■ In a big pot bring water to a boil. Remove the squash from the skin to a mixing bowl (or a food processor) with the garlic cloves and puree to a smooth paste. Check for flavor and season if needed.

■ Arrange 6 skins on a working surface and place a teaspoon of the filling in the middle of three of them. Brush the other three with egg white around the edges and place them on top of the one with the filling. Seal the edges well using your index finger and thumb. Four raviolis per person is the equivalent of one portion.

■ When the water is boiling, add salt and then cook the raviolis for 1-2 minutes. Remove to a strainer.

■ Season the racks with salt and freshly ground black pepper. Sear in hot oil on all sides. Remove from the pan and place on a baking sheet.

■ Roast racks in oven until rare-medium rare (lamb should be 125-130 degrees), approximately 15 minutes.

■ Combine the bread, olive oil and herbs in a food processor and blend well. Remove lamb from oven, and smear with mustard. Coat with breadcrumb mixture. Return to oven and cook another 2 minutes, or until crumbs are lightly toasted.

■ Allow the lamb to rest for 10 minutes before carving. Carve and serve immediately with the raviolis. Drizzle the vinaigrette.

LAMB SHOULDER WITH DRIED FRUIT STUFFING AND SAUTÉED HARICOT VERT
Serves 4-6

1 lamb shoulder, boned and butterflied (about 3 pounds)
4 slices Challa bread, or raisin bread, diced
3 ounces walnuts, broken
3 ounces dried apricots, diced
3 ounces prunes, pitted and roughly chopped
6-8 garlic cloves
2 tablespoons olive oil + 2 more for sautéing bread
1 teaspoon fresh thyme leaves
1/2 teaspoon grated nutmeg
Salt and pepper
1/4 cup olive oil
1 bottle semi-dry white wine
1 pound haricot vert
2 tablespoons extra virgin olive oil
1/2 cup sliced, toasted almonds
butcher twine

DOLLY

SHEEP FACSIMILE. The young lamb named Dolly (left), with her surrogate mother, was created by cloning at the Roslin Institute.

Preheat oven to 375 degrees F.

- Place the garlic cloves and 2 tablespoons olive oil in aluminum foil and close tightly. Bake for 20–25 minutes until cloves are golden and soft. Keep the oil.

- In a wide sauté pan heat the 2 tablespoons of oil with the 'garlic" oil and sauté the bread until golden brown and crispy.

- Mix the dried fruits, nuts, bread, garlic, thyme, nutmeg, salt and pepper.

- Spread the stuffing on the butterflied shoulder (nice side down), roll to a tight roulade tacking the sides inwards (like a warp). Tie with butcher twine. Season well with salt and pepper.

- Heat the 1/4 cup olive oil in a wide sauté pan and sear the roulade from all sides. Remove to a roasting pan and add the wine to the hot sauté pan. Bring to a boil and pour over the roulade. Braise in the oven for 1 hour. Remove from the liquids and let stand for 10 minutes before slicing into portions.

- Cook the haricot vert in salted boiling water for 2 minutes then immediately remove to a bowl with iced water. Let cool for 3 minutes and drain.

- Heat the oil in a sauté pan and sauté the haricot vert for 2 minutes. Toss with the almonds and season with salt.

- Fan the lamb slices on a plate and pile the haricot vert in the middle. Drizzle with the sauce and serve.

VENISON FILLETS IN POMEGRANATE SAUCE OVER ROASTED PARSNIP, APPLE PUREE AND WATERCRESS SALAD

Serves 4

PAN-SEARED RIB EYE STEAK WITH PORT & BALSAMIC REDUCTION SAUCE OVER BEET AND POTATO LATKES

Serves 4

4 8-ounce rib eye steaks
1 large baking potato peeled and coarsely grated
2 medium (4 ounces) red beets, peeled and coarsely grated
2 small yellow onions, coarsely grated
2 large eggs, lightly beaten
1/2 cup flour
1 teaspoon salt
Freshly ground black pepper to taste
2/3 cup Canola oil
1/2 teaspoon crushed red peppercorns
1/2 teaspoon crushed green peppercorns
1/2 teaspoon crushed black peppercorns
1 teaspoon crushed sea salt
3 tablespoons duck fat or olive oil
1/2 bottle port
1/2 bottle balsamic vinegar
2 cups veal or beef stock
2 shallots, chopped
1 tablespoon olive oil
2 radicchios, each cut into 6
3 tablespoons olive oil
Salt and pepper

Preparation – Latkes:

■ Rinse the grated potatoes in a bowl of cold water. Remove the potatoes, shred with your fingers on a clean kitchen towel. Roll up in the towel and squeeze dry. Place the beets and onions in a large colander and strongly squeeze out the excess moisture.

■ In a bowl, stir together the potato, beets, onion, eggs, flour, salt, and pepper to taste. Heat 1/3 cup of the Canola oil in a cast-iron skillet over medium-high heat. Add 4 heaping tablespoons of batter to the pan to form 4 pancakes; flatten slightly. Cook for about 5 minutes, turning once, until golden brown on both sides. Keep warm on a rack set over a baking sheet in a low oven. Repeat with the remaining potato mixture and the rest of the oil.

■ Rub the radicchio slices in oil, season with salt and pepper and grill in a grill pan for 2 minutes on each side. Keep warm.

■ Mix all peppers and sea salt. Rub the steaks on both sides with the pepper mixture.

■ In a wide saucepan heat the olive oil; sauté the shallots for 30 seconds (until translucent); add the wine, port and stock. Bring to a boil and reduce to a simmer. Reduce by two thirds until sauce is thick and coats a spoon. In a big sauté pan heat the fat and sear the meat for 2-3 minutes on both sides. Transfer to a serving plate and drizzle the sauce. Serve with the latkes and grilled radicchios.

HORSERADISH MUSTARD-CRUSTED ROAST BEEF WITH WARM POTATO SALAD AND GRILLED TOMATOES

Serves 6-8

3 pounds eye round roast, cleaned

1 cup grainy horseradish flavored Dijon mustard

2 sprigs rosemary

Butcher twine

3 tablespoons Canola oil

3 pounds bliss potatoes

3 ounces olive oil

2 ounces cider vinegar

2 tablespoons minced shallots

1 1/2 tablespoons Dijon mustard

1 tablespoon chopped parsley

1 1/2 tablespoons chopped tarragon

1 1/2 teaspoons sugar

1/2 teaspoon salt

1/2 teaspoon ground black pepper

2 beefsteak tomatoes

2 tablespoons olive oil

1 teaspoon fresh thyme leaves

Salt and pepper

Preheat oven to 475 degrees F.

Preparation – Salad:

■ Place the potatoes in a pot and cover with water. Bring to a boil and cook until tender. Strain and let cool. When cool enough to handle slice 1/4-inch thick.

■ In a large bowl, whisk together the olive oil, vinegar, shallots and mustard. Add the parsley, tarragon, sugar, salt and pepper. Gently toss the potatoes in the dressing and keep warm.

Season the meat well with salt and pepper and tie in a tight ov shape with the butcher twine.

■ Spread the mustard generously all over the meat and place on sprig of rosemary on each side, lengthwise, using the twig to ho it in place.

■ Heat a wide sauté pan or a cast iron skillet for 3-5 minutes. Ad the oil and sear the meat on all sides. Remove the meat to roasting rack and place in the oven. Roast for 40-45 minutes. Th internal temperature should be 135 (medium rare). Let stand for 1

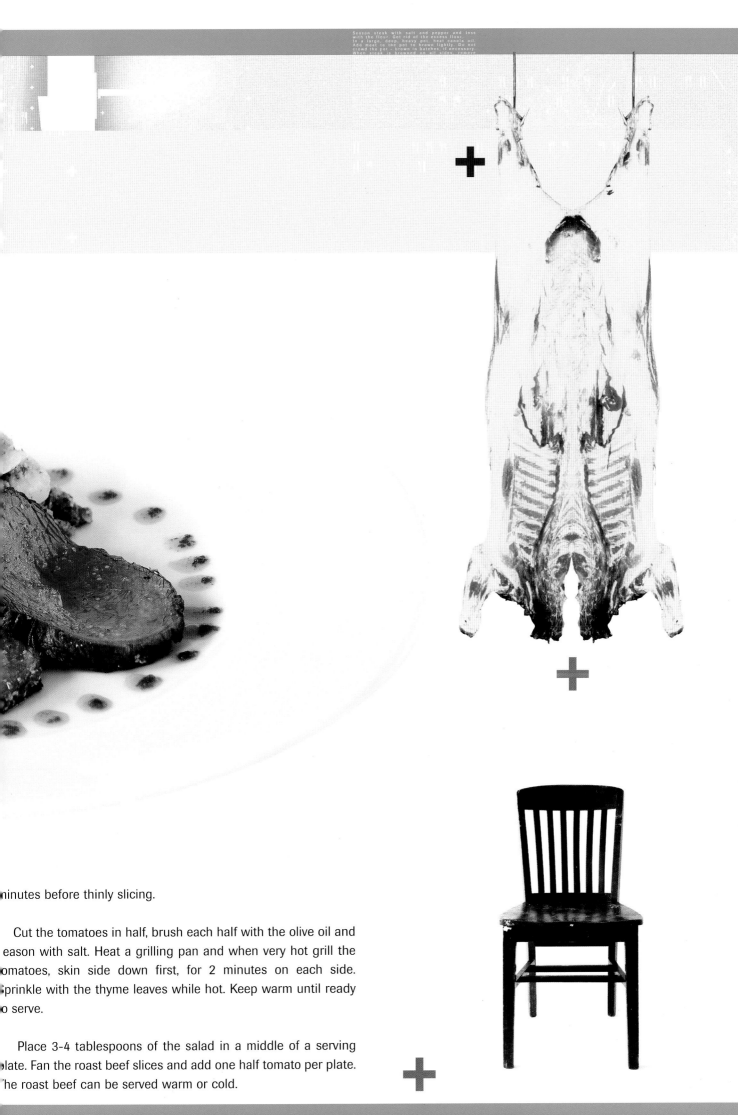

minutes before thinly slicing.

Cut the tomatoes in half, brush each half with the olive oil and season with salt. Heat a grilling pan and when very hot grill the tomatoes, skin side down first, for 2 minutes on each side. Sprinkle with the thyme leaves while hot. Keep warm until ready to serve.

Place 3-4 tablespoons of the salad in a middle of a serving plate. Fan the roast beef slices and add one half tomato per plate. The roast beef can be served warm or cold.

LAMB KABOBS WITH GREEN TAHINI SAUCE, TOMATO SALAD AND PITA BREAD POINTS

Serves 4

For the Kabobs:

2 pounds ground lamb meat
1/2 cup chopped parsley
2 garlic cloves, chopped
1/3 cup chopped onions
1 teaspoon Baharat (Mediterranean seasoning)
Salt and pepper
3 tablespoons lamb or duck fat

For the Tahini:

1 cup Tahini paste
1/3 cup lemon juice
1/2 cup water
2 garlic cloves
2/3 cup parsley, chopped
1/3 cup cilantro leaves
Salt and pepper

4 ripe but firm tomatoes
2 tablespoons extra virgin olive oil
1/4 cup chopped fresh mint leaves
1 tablespoon lemon juice
2-3 pita breads
2 tablespoons olive oil
1 garlic clove, halved

Preheat oven to 350 degrees F.

■ Mix all the kabob ingredients, but the fat. Make finger-long patties out of the meat and keep in the refrigerator for half an hour.

Preparation — Tahini

■ In a food processor, mix the tahini, lemon juice and water. Purée for 1 minute. Add the garlic and herbs and purée for 20 seconds until herbs are well chopped. Season well with salt and pepper and set aside until ready to serve.

■ Take the green tip off the tomatoes, cut into quarters and discard the seeds. Dice each quarter and mix with the olive oil, lemon juice and mint. Season with salt and keep refrigerated until serving time.

■ Cut the pita bread, horizontally, to create 2 discs. Brush the discs with the olive oil and rub with the garlic. Cut each disc into 8 triangles and toast in the oven for 5-7 minutes.

■ Heat the fat in a sauté pan. Fry the kabobs 2 minutes on each side until brown and crisp but medium in the middle. Arrange on a plate and drizzle with green tahini. Serve with pita bread points and chopped tomato salad.

VEAL SCALOPPINE IN CURRY SAUCE WITH STEAMED WHITE RICE
Serves 4

8 veal scaloppine (2 per person), about 2 pounds
3 tablespoons flour
1 tablespoon and 1 teaspoon good quality curry powder
1 1/2 teaspoon salt
3 tablespoons canola oil
1/2 cup dry white wine
1/2 cup coconut milk
1 tablespoon lemon juice
1/3 cup chopped cilantro for garnish
2/3 cups coconut flakes (unsweetened), toasted in the
oven until lightly golden and crisp
4 zucchini
2 tablespoons olive oil
1 teaspoon fresh thyme leaves
2 cups jasmine rice

■ Place the rice in a strainer and rinse under cool water until the ter runs clear, about 2 minutes. Drain thoroughly.

■ Place 2/3 cups of water, the rice, and the salt in a 2-quart pot. ng to a boil over medium-high heat, uncovered, then cover and mmer for 18 minutes. Fluff the rice with a fork and keep hot until ving.

■ Place the scaloppine between two plastic wrap sheets and pound enly until 1/8-inch thick. Mix the flour with the teaspoon of curry d salt. Dredge the scaloppine in the flour and curry mixture and ake to get rid of the excess flour.

■ Heat the oil in a sauté pan and fry the scaloppine a minute on each side. Do not overcrowd the pan; fry in batches if needed. Remove from the pan and set aside.

■ Add the rest of the curry to the pan and scorch the bottom with a wooden spoon, add the wine, lemon and coconut milk. Cook while mixing for about 5 minutes and season with salt if needed.

■ Return the scaloppine to the pan and cook with the sauce for 2-3 minutes. Transfer to a serving plate and garnish with the chopped cilantro and toasted coconut flakes.

ROUND STEAK ROLLUPS WITH VERMOUTH SAUCE, SAUTÉED LEEKS AND BUTTON MUSHROOM
Serves 4

- Cut meat into 8 pieces and pound until 1/4-inch thick.

- In a sauté pan, heat the olive oil and sauté the onion for 1 minute, until translucent. Add the butternut squash and sauté for 3-4 minutes. Add the peppers and celery, sauté for 1 minute. Season with thyme leaves, salt and pepper. Mix in breadcrumbs.

- Combine flour, 1 teaspoon salt, and pepper. Dredge each piece of meat in the seasoned flour.

- Spread squash mixture evenly over each piece of meat, roll and fasten with a toothpick. Brown meat rolls on all sides in 1/4 cup

margarine in a wide sauté pan. Remove the roulades from the pan. Add stock, Vermouth and pearl onion to the pan. Bring to a boil and reduce to a simmer. Cook until reduced by half and thickened. Add rollups and cook for 2 minutes.

- In a wide sauté pan or a wok, heat the oil. Add the leeks and stir-fry for 2 minutes. Add the mushrooms and stir constantly over high flame. Add the Vermouth and season with salt. Cook for 1 more minute.

- Spread the sautéed vegetables on a serving plate and place two rollups in the center in an X shape. Drizzle with the sauce and serve.

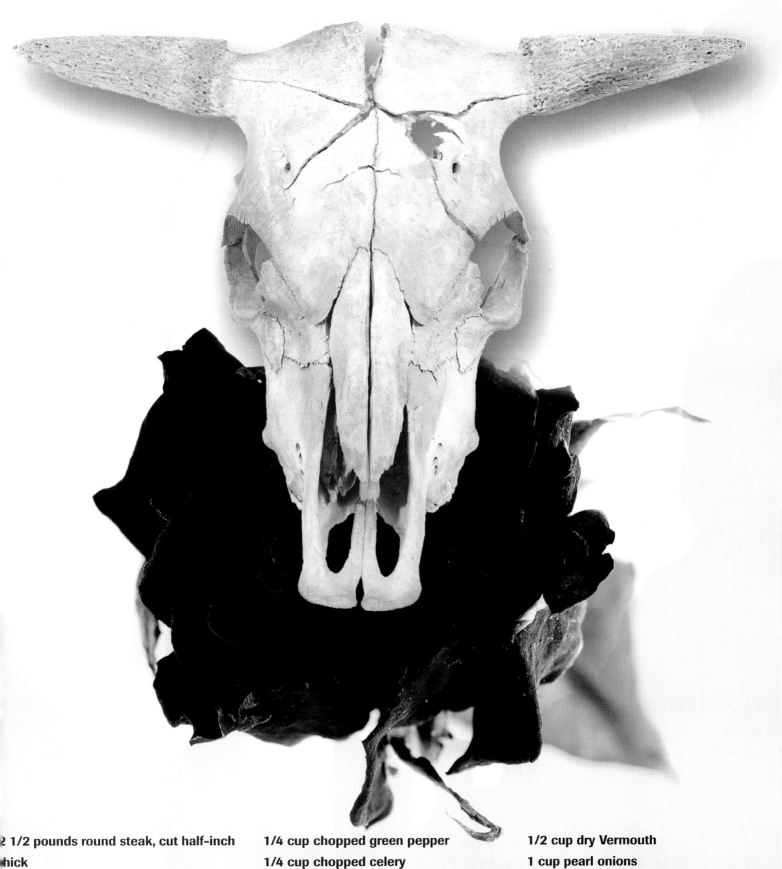

257

2 1/2 pounds round steak, cut half-inch thick

1 cup flour

1 teaspoon salt

1/2 teaspoon pepper

1 cup fresh bread crumbs

1 1/4 cups chopped onion

2 cups diced butternut squash (peeled)

1/4 cup chopped green pepper

1/4 cup chopped celery

2 tablespoons olive oil

1 tablespoon fresh thyme leaves

1 teaspoon salt

1 egg, beaten

1/4 cup margarine

1 cup beef stock

1/2 cup dry Vermouth

1 cup pearl onions

1/2 pound button mushroom, quartered

3 leeks, white part only, washed and sliced to 1/8-inch slices

2 tablespoons grapeseed oil

1/4 cup Vermouth

Salt

STIR FRIED BEEF WITH SUN DRIED TOMATOES OVER ORZO PRIMAVERA
Serves 4

1 pound London broil, thinly sliced

5 ounces sun dried tomatoes in oil, drained (keep the oil)
and sliced

3 tablespoons olive oil

1 red onion, chopped

2 garlic cloves, chopped

1 big tomato, diced

1-2 zucchinis (6 ounces), thinly sliced

1/3 cup black Kalamata olives, pitted

1 tablespoon chopped fresh rosemary leaves

2 teaspoons tomato paste

1 1/2 cups chicken or beef stock

1/3 cup dry white wine

1 teaspoon cornstarch mixed in 2 tablespoons water

Salt and pepper

1/2 cup chopped parsley for garnish

1/2 pound orzo

1 cup carrot, julienne

1/2 red pepper, julienne

1/2 cup scallions

1/2 cup cherry tomatoes, halved

2 tablespoons fresh basil, julienne

1/4 cup chopped fresh flat leaf parsley

2 tablespoons Canola oil

eat salted water in a large saucepan. Add the orzo and cook until
ente, about 8 minutes. Drain, rinse and set aside.

Meanwhile heat the oil in a sauté pan and sauté the carrots and
pers for 2-3 minutes until crisp and tender. Add the tomatoes and
ions and cook for 1 minute. Mix the orzo with the vegetables and
s. Season with salt and pepper.

eason the meat slices with salt and pepper.

a wok or a wide sauté pan heat 2 tablespoons of the sun-dried

tomatoes in oil. Stir-fry the meat, mixing well, for 2 minutes. Remove
from the pan and set aside. Add the olive oil and fry the onions, garlic
and zucchinis for 1 minute. Add the tomato dices and olives and fry
for 2 additional minutes.

■   Add the wine, stock and cornstarch mixture and cook for 10
minutes, mixing occasionally. Add the sun-dried tomatoes and the
meat and cook for 2 minutes.

■ Place 4 tablespoons of the orzo in the middle of a wide soup bowl
and top with the stir-fried beef. Garnish with parsley leaves and serve.

PECAN-CRUSTED VEAL MEDALLIONS OVER BARLEY RISOTTO WITH ONION JAM AND BASIL OIL

Serves 4

11/2 pounds veal loin cleaned and cut into half-inch medallions
2 cups finely chopped pecan nuts (not roasted)
Pinch cayenne pepper
1 egg, beaten
1/3 cup flour
Salt and pepper

2 tablespoons Canola oil
4 medium onions, thinly sliced
1/2 cup brown sugar
2 tablespoons balsamic vinegar
2 tablespoons olive oil
Salt and pepper

Preparation — Jam:

■ In a saucepot heat the oil and add the onions. Reduce to medium-low heat and let cook, stirring occasionally, for about 20 minutes until onions have softened. Add the vinegar and sugar and cook for 5 minutes until sugar dissolves. Reduce to low heat and cook for 45 minutes until all liquids are gone and the jam is a dark brown color. Season with salt and pepper and keep warm until serving. (Jam can be made in advance, kept in the refrigerator and used when needed.)

Preparation — Oil:

■ Chop the basil leaves well. Transfer to a food processor, add the canola oil and blend together. Transfer to a squeezing bottle.

Preparation — Risotto:

■ Heat the stock in a large saucepan over medium heat until it come to a boil. Reduce heat to low, keeping the stock at a steady simmer.

■ Heat the oil in heavy-bottomed saucepan over medium heat. Ad the shallots, and cook until translucent, about 4 minutes. Add th barley, and cook, stirring with a wooden spoon, until the rice is coate in the oil and the kernels are translucent, about 3 minutes.

■ Add the wine, and cook, stirring, until all the wine is absorbed Ladle 3/4 cup of the hot stock into the barley, stirring constantly unt

1/2 cup Canola oil
7 ounces basil leaves, washed and dried
6-7 cups vegetable stock
3 tablespoons extra virgin olive oil
2 large shallots, finely chopped
1 1/2 cups pearl barley

1/2 cup dry white wine
4 tablespoons margarine, cut in pieces
1/4 cup chopped fresh flat-leaf parsley
Salt and pepper

most of the liquid has been absorbed, and the mixture is just thick enough to leave a clear wake behind when a line is drawn through the mixture, about 3 minutes. Continue adding stock in this manner (about 3/4 cup at a time), stirring constantly, until all the stock has been used up, the barley is fully cooked, and it is suspended in a liquid that resembles heavy cream – a total of about 20 minutes.

■ Remove risotto from heat, and add the margarine pieces and parsley, stirring until melted and combined, about 1 minute. Season with salt and pepper.

Preheat oven to 450 degrees F.
■ Mix the nuts with the cayenne pepper. Season the medallions with

salt and pepper. Dredge one side in the flour and then in the egg and chopped nuts (so only one side is crusted).

■ Heat the canola oil in a wide sauté pan and sauté the medallions crust side down for 1 minute. Gently turn over and sauté for 3 minutes. Transfer the pan to the oven for 5 minutes (internal temperature should be 150 degrees F).

■ Serve over a little of the onion jam, with grilled polenta and arugula or basil oil.

BEEF AND PEAR SKEWERS OVER CRISPY SWEET POTATOES AND GREENS

Serves 4

1 1/2 pounds rib eye, cleaned and diced one-inch thick
3 Bosc pears, washed, seeded and diced one-inch thick
1 medium Vidalia onion or any sweet onion, diced one-inch thick

For the Marinade:

2 shallots, chopped
2 garlic cloves, minced
3 tablespoons good quality pear liquor, apple liqueur or a good brandy
3 tablespoons grape seed oil
2 tablespoons cider vinegar
1 tablespoon honey
2 tablespoons chopped fresh tarragon leaves
Salt and pepper
3 medium sweet potatoes, washed but not peeled
1/4 cup olive oil
2 tablespoons chopped fresh sage leaves

Mix all of the marinade ingredients in a bowl. Rub the meat dices in the marinade, cover with plastic wrap and leave in the fridge for at least hours (up to 24 hours) mixing the meat every few hours (the marinade should not cover the meat completely).

Preparation – Potatoes:

Preheat oven to 375 degrees F.

Using a mandolin, or a very sharp knife, slice the sweet potatoes into very thin slices. Gently toss them in the oil and sage and season with salt. Arrange them, overlapping, in a baking dish and cover with aluminum foil. Bake for 30 minutes. Remove the foil and bake for 20-25 additional minutes until crispy.

■ Strain the meat from the marinade (keep the marinade left over) and thread on metal skewers (if using wooden ones soak them in water for 15 minutes before using) alternating with pear and onion dices. Brush with the marinade liquids and season lightly with salt and pepper.

■ Grill over a hot grill, griddle or grilling pan for 3 minutes on each side. Arrange the sweet potato crisps on a serving plate, lean 3 skewers on top and top with green salad.

BRAISED SHORT RIBS WITH GARLIC MASHED POTATOES AND SAUTÉED BABY SPINACH

Serves 4

Preheat oven to 375 degrees F.

■ Mix all marinade ingredients and pour over ribs. Cover and place in the refrigerator for 12 hours or up to 2 days.

■ Remove ribs from refrigerator and pat dry. Toss the marinade.

■ In a big braising pot heat the oil and sear the ribs on both sides (do not overcrowd the pan, prepare 2 batches if needed). Remov from the pan and set aside. Sauté the vegetables and garlic for minutes, add the wine and bring to a boil. Add the ribs and herb cover and place in the oven. Braise for 2 hours until meat is ver soft.

■ Place the garlic cloves on a square of aluminum foil and drizzl with a little of the extra virgin olive oil. Close the sides of the foil t

265

pounds short ribs (2-3 per person)

For the Marinade:

bottle red wine (Cabernet Sauvignon)
cup diced onions
/2 cup diced carrots
/2 cup diced celery stalks
garlic cloves, sliced
sprigs thyme
sprigs parsley
bay leaves

For the Sauce:

1 bottle red wine (Cabernet Sauvignon)
1 cup diced onions
1/2 cup diced carrots
1/2 cup diced celery stalks
1/2 cup diced parsnips
6 garlic cloves, sliced
1 sprig thyme
1 sprig parsley
1 bay leaf

3 tablespoons olive oil
4-5 Idaho potatoes, peeled and diced half-inch thick
10 garlic cloves, peeled
1/4 -1/3 cup high quality extra virgin olive oil + 1 tablespoon
Salt and pepper
1 pound baby spinach, washed and dried
2 tablespoons olive oil

eate a sealed pocket and place in the oven for 20-25 minutes until ꞁlden and soft.

Cook the potato dices in salted water (not covered) until soft but ꞁt falling apart. Transfer to a strainer and let stand for 5 minutes. ꞁree the potatoes with the garlic using a food mill or a masher ꞁhile drizzling the 1/4 cup of oil; use the rest only if the mashed

potatoes are still dry. Season well with salt and keep warm.
Heat the oil in a sauté pan. Add the spinach, season with salt and cook for 30 seconds over a high flame.

■ Arrange the mashed potatoes toward the side of the serving plate, lean 2-3 ribs against it, cover the ribs with sauce and top with the sautéed spinach.

CLUB STEAK WITH HERBED ISRAELI COUSCOUS AND STUFFED JAPANESE EGGPLANT

Serves 4

4 8-ounce club steaks 1 inch thick
Salt and pepper
2 garlic cloves, halved
2 tablespoons Canola oil or duck fat

For the Couscous:

1 package Israeli couscous
1 cup chopped parsley leaves
1/3 cup chopped mint leaves
1/3 cup chopped chives
2 roasted red peppers, diced

small
3 tablespoons olive oil
Salt and pepper

For the Sauce:

1 small onion, diced
1 carrot, diced

Preparation — Sauce:

■ In a saucepot, heat the olive oil and sauté the vegetables for 2 minutes. Add the stock, garlic and herbs. Bring to a boil and reduce to a simmer. Let reduce by 2/3 until the stock thickens and is dark brown. If using a demi glass just bring to a boil and let simmer for 5 minutes. Strain and keep warm until serving.

Preparation — Eggplants:

■ Preheat oven to 350 degrees F. With a peeler, peel stripe lengthwise of the eggplants. Heat the oil and deep-fry the eggplant whole, for 3 minutes. Transfer to a plate lined with paper towels to g rid of excess fat. When cold enough to handle cut a slit in the midd of the eggplant, but not all the way through, to create a pocket.

celery stalks, diced
garlic head, halved
tablespoons olive oil
bay leaf
sprigs fresh thyme
/2 sprig rosemary
quarts good beef stock or 2

cups demi glass (reduced beef stock)

For the eggplants:
4 Japanese eggplants
Vegetable oil for deep-frying
2 big tomatoes, diced

1 big yellow onion, cut in half and sliced
1 teaspoon thyme leaves
1/4 cup chopped basil leaves
1/2 cup roasted pine nuts
Salt and pepper

In a wide sauté pan heat the oil and sauté the onion slices for 4 inutes. Add the tomatoes and herbs, season with salt and pepper nd cook for 5 minutes. Mix in the pine nuts and remove from the eat. Season the inside of the eggplants with salt and pepper and uff the pockets with the tomatoes and onion mixture. Place on a aking sheet and bake in the oven for 30 minutes.

Preparation – Israeli Couscous:

■ Cook the couscous following the directions on the package. Drain.
In a wide sauté pan heat the olive oil, add the couscous and stir constantly to coat with the oil. Add the diced roasted peppers and season with salt and pepper. Add the herbs and mix well. Check for flavor.

WHEN YOU INVEST A LOT IN COOKING YOUR
FOOD, THE PRESENTATION SHOULD REFLECT
THAT INVESTMENT.

DESSERTS

SEMOLINA CAKE DIAMONDS WITH NUT TOPPING AND HONEY-FLAVORED YOGURT

Serves 4

A Tribute To Stanley Kubrick s
A Clockwork Orange

4 ounces unsalted butter, softened
1/2 cup sugar
1 cup semolina
1 cup ground roasted hazelnuts
1 tablespoon baking powder
3 eggs, lightly beaten
1/2 tablespoon orange zest
1/2 tablespoon lemon zest
2 tablespoons orange juice

For the Syrup

3 cups sugar
3 cups water
2 cinnamon sticks
1 star anise
2 whole cloves
1 tablespoon orange rind, julienne
1/3 cup lemon juice
1/2 cup orange blossom water

For the Topping

1/2 cup roasted slivered almonds
1/2 cup roasted hazelnuts, coarsely
chopped
1 cup plain yogurt
1 tablespoon honey
Lavender flowers for garnish

Preheat oven to 415 degrees F.

■ Lightly grease a 9-inch square baking pan and line the base with parchment paper. Cream the butter and sugar in a medium bowl until light and fluffy. Stir in the semolina, ground hazelnuts and baking powder. Add the eggs one by one, orange rind, juice and fold thoroughly until well combined. Spoon into the pan, smooth the surface and bake for 20 minutes, or until golden and set. Leave in the tin.

Preparation – Syrup:

■ Place the sugar, cinnamon sticks, star anise, cloves and 3 cups water in a saucepan over low heat and stir until the sugar has dissolved. Increase the heat and boil rapidly, without stirring, for 5 minutes. Pour into a heatproof measuring jug then return half to saucepan. Let simmer for 15-20 minutes, or until thickened and reduced to to 2/3 of a cup. Stir in the orange and lemon zest.

■ Add the lemon juice and orange blossom water to the syrup in the jug, and pour it over the cake in the tin. When absorbed, turn the cake out onto a large flat plate. Slice into 4 equal strips, then slice each strip diagonally into 3 diamond-shaped pieces. Discard the ends.

Preparation – Topping:

■ Combine the almonds and hazelnuts and scatter over the cake. Pour the thickened syrup and julienne orange rind over the nuts. Let stand for 30 minutes before serving.

■ Gently transfer the diamonds to individual plates. In a small mixing bowl briefly combine the yogurt with the honey and place a tablespoon on each plate. Sprinkle with lavender flowers and serve.

BAKLAVA
Serves 6-8

2 1/2 cups sugar

2 teaspoons lemon zest

1/4 cup honey

2 teaspoons lemon juice

2 tablespoons orange blossom water

7 ounces walnuts, finely chopped

7 ounces shelled pistachios, finely chopped

6 1/2 ounces almonds, finely chopped

2 tablespoons sugar

2 teaspoons ground cinnamon

6 1/2 ounces unsalted butter, melted

12 ounces filo pastry

Preheat oven to 325 degrees F.

■ Place the sugar, lemon rind and 1 1/2 cups water in a saucepan and stir over high heat until the sugar is dissolved, boil for 5 minutes. Reduce heat and let simmer for 5 minutes, or until the syrup has thickened slightly and coats the back of a spoon. Add the honey, lemon juice and orange blossom water and cook for 2 minutes. Remove from the heat and leave to cool completely.

■ Combine the nuts, extra sugar and cinnamon in a bowl. Brush the base and sides of a 12 x 11-inch baking dish or tin with melted butter. Cover the base with a single layer of filo pastry, brush lightly with butter, folding in any overhanging edges. Continue layering the filo, brushing each new layer with butter and folding in the edges until 10 sheets have been used. Keep the unused filo under a damp tea towel.

■ Sprinkle half the nut mixture over the pastry and pat down evenly. Repeat the layering and buttering of 5 more filo sheets, sprinkle with the remaining nuts, then continue to layer and butter the remaining sheets, including the top layer. Press down with your hands so the pastry and nuts stick to each other. Using a large sharp knife, cut them into diamond shapes, ensuring you cut through the bottom layer. Pour any remaining butter evenly over the top and smooth with your hands. Bake for 30 minutes, then lower the temperature to 300 degrees F, and bake for another 30 minutes.

■ Immediately cut through the original diamond markings then strain the syrup evenly over the top. Cool completely before lifting the diamonds out onto a serving platter.

(It is important for the baklava to be piping hot and the syrup cold when pouring the syrup.)

PISTACHIO CREME AND BLACKBERRY ROLLS WITH MINT CREME FRAICHE

Serves 6-8

2 sheets (1 package) high quality puff pastry
3 ounces butter
3 ounces granulated sugar
1/2 teaspoon grated lemon zest
1 whole egg + 1 egg yolk
1/2 teaspoon vanilla extract
5 ounces shelled, unsalted pistachios
2 tablespoons flour
2 pints blackberries
1 container (8 ounces) creme fraiche
7 mint leaves, washed and dried

Preheat oven to 400 degrees F.

■ Grease and flour 12 muffin tins. Mix 3 ounces of the pistachios with the flour in a food processor until finely ground (should look like breadcrumbs).

■ Place the butter, lemon zest and sugar in a mixer bowl with the pedal attachment and cream until pale and light. Beat the egg, egg yolk and vanilla together and add them gradually to the creamed butter while mixing. Stir in the granulated pistachios.

■ Spread one of the puff pastry sheets on a lightly floured surface and roll it briefly into a 1/8-inch thick rectangle. Spread half of the pistachio cream on the sheet leaving a narrow strip (about 1 inch) uncovered on the top edge. Sprinkle with 1/2 pint of the black berries, saving the rest for garnish.

■ Starting from the bottom edge, roll the dough tightly and even into a cylinder. To keep filling intact, do not squeeze. Repeat with th other sheet.

■ Using a bench knife, or a very sharp knife, cut the cylinder into 6 7 rolls and place each roll into a muffin tin. Bake for about 20 minute until golden and fully baked in the middle. Roast the 2 ounces pistachios in the oven for about 5 minutes, let cool.

■ Place the creme fraiche and the mint leaves in a fine sieve and us a spoon to mash them through the sieve into a bowl (best to use light green cream).

■ Unmold the pastries. Place one pastry per person on a servin plate and add a small dollop of the mint cream next to it. Sprinkl around with a few blackberries and the roasted pistachios and serve

ROSE WATER & VANILLA PANNA COTTA WITH STRAWBERRY SAUCE
Serves 6

4 cups heavy cream
1/2 cup sugar
1 vanilla bean or 1 teaspoon vanilla extract
2 tablespoons rose water
2 1/2 teaspoons gelatin powder
2 tablespoons water

For the Sauce:
1 cup strawberries, washed and cut in halves
Cheesecloth (optional)
1/3 cup sugar
Rose petals for garnish

■ Mix sugar and cream in a saucepot; split the vanilla bean in half and scrape the seeds into the cream and sugar mixture; throw the vanilla bean in as well. Bring the cream to a boil, mixing well, and reduce heat to a light simmer. Let simmer for 45 minutes.

■ Place gelatin and water in a small saucepan and heat briefly. Stir well until the entire gelatin has dissolved.

■ Strain the cream and add a little of it to the gelatin. Combine both mixtures, then add the rose water and whisk well. Pour into small serving dishes and refrigerate for 4 hours (until set).

■ Blend strawberries and sugar in a food processor to achieve a liquid texture. To get rid of the seeds strain the sauce through the cheesecloth.

■ Remove the panna cotta from the mold and transfer to a plate. Pour around with sauce, garnish with fresh strawberries and the rose petals. Serve.

MANGO TARTE TATIN
Serves 6

1 1/2 cups all purpose flour
5 ounces cold butter, diced small
A pinch of salt
1/3 cup sugar
2-3 tablespoons cold water
4 firm mangoes
1 cup sugar
2.5 ounces butter

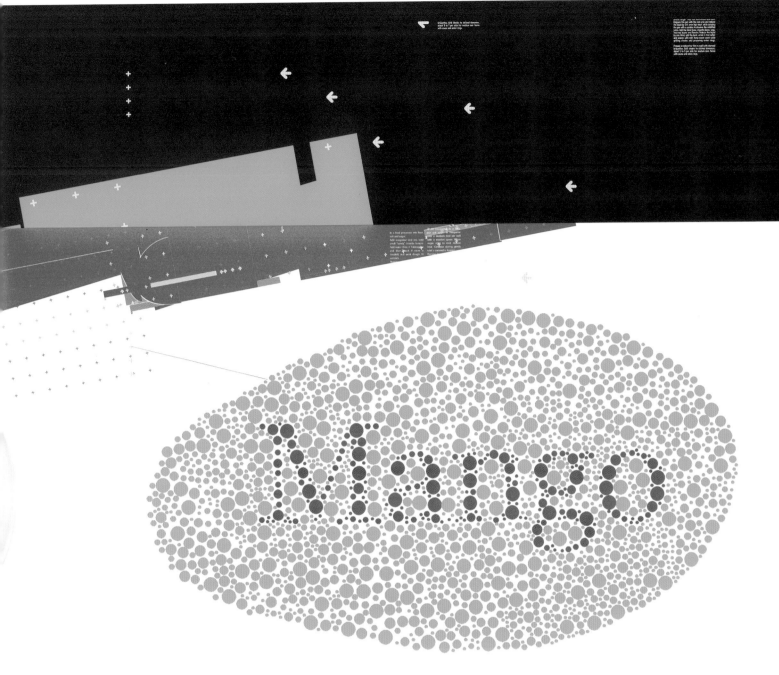

Heat oven to 350 degrees F.

■ Mix flour, salt and sugar in a food processor. Add margarine and mix until a small "sandy" crumb texture is achieved. Add water (first 2 tablespoons and more if needed) and work dough for 10 seconds. Remove the dough to a working surface and, with fast movements, create a bowl. Flatten the bowl of dough to a disc shape and place in the refrigerator for 20 minutes.

■ In the meantime, put sugar and margarine in a cake pan over a medium heat and stir well with a wooden spoon. When sugar begins to melt, reduce heat. Continue stirring gently until a caramel is formed. Remove from heat and let cool.

■ Peel the mangoes and slice them half-inch thick. Arrange in the pan, overlapping. Roll dough to fit the cake pan and place it over the mango. Bake for 40 minutes. Let cool and when still warm turn the cake upside down to a serving platter. Serve warm!

FLOURLESS CHOCOLATE MOUSSE CAKE WITH RASPBERRY COULIS

Serves 6

Preheat the oven to 325 degrees F.

Preparation – Base:

■ Melt the chocolate and butter gently over a double boiler. Remove from the heat and sift in the cocoa powder. Add the yolks, one at a time, and mix well. Place the egg whites in a mixer bowl with the cream of tartar, sugar and salt and beat to a soft pick stage. Gently fold the whites into the chocolate. Bake for 40 minutes. Let cool.

Preparation – Mousse:

■ Melt the chocolate slowly over a double boiler. Add the egg and mix well with a wooden spoon (the chocolate should be warm but not too hot). Remove from the heat. Whip the heavy cream until gently whipped and fold into the chocolate. Pour over the base, spread evenly and refrigerate.

■ Place the water and sugar in a small saucepan over a low heat and mix until the sugar dissolves. Add the raspberries and cook for 3 minutes. Transfer to a blender and purée for 1 minute. Strain through a fine sieve and keep refrigerated until serving.

For the Base:
9 ounces bittersweet chocolate, chopped
4 ounces butter
5 eggs, separated
1 tablespoon cocoa powder
1/2 cup sugar
Pinch cream of tartar
Pinch of salt

For the Chocolate Mousse:
8 ounces bittersweet chocolate
1 egg
2 1/2 cups heavy cream
1 pint raspberries + raspberries for garnish
1/4 cup water
2 tablespoons sugar

HALVA PARFAIT WITH CHOCOLATE CARDAMOM SAUCE

Serves 6

12 ounces good quality plain halva
6 eggs, separated
1/4 cup sugar
2 cups heavy cream
4 ounces bittersweet chocolate, chopped
1/2 teaspoon round cardamom
4 ounces heavy cream
Fresh mint leaves for garnish

■ Crumble the halva and place in a mixer bowl with the whisk attachment. Add the egg yolks and mix to a smooth thick texture. Remove from the bowl to a big mixing bowl. Place the egg whites in a clean dried mixer bowl. Beat the whites and the sugar to a soft peak stage, fold third of the egg whites into the halva mixture and then fold the rest of the whites. Do not overmix.

■ Whip the heavy cream and fold into the halva mixture. Transfer to a loaf pan, big enough to hold the parfait and place in the freezer for at least 4 hours or overnight.

Preparation — Sauce:

■ Heat the heavy cream and the cardamom until almost boiling and pour over the chopped chocolate. Let stand for 5 minutes and mix well. Transfer to a squeeze bottle.

■ Drizzle the chocolate sauce in a web pattern on a wide plate. Run warm water on the outside of the parfait dish and unmold onto a cutting board. Run a knife blade under hot water, dry with a towel and cut the parfait while the blade is still hot, 2 slices (1/4 inch) per serving. Place the slices, one leaning on the other, in the middle of the plate; garnish with the mint leaves and serve.

GINGER LEMON PERSONAL TARTLETS WITH CRÈME DE CASSIS CHANTILLY
Serves 6

For the Dough:

2 cups all purpose flour

6 ounces butter, diced small and chilled

1/4 cup sugar

Pinch salt

1/4 cup heavy cream

For the Filling:

1 tablespoon chopped fresh ginger

2 1/2 cups whole milk

3 ounces sugar

2 ounces cornstarch

6 egg yolks

Parchment paper

Beans or lentils to weigh down the dough (blind baking)

1 cup freshly squeezed lemon juice

Zest of 1 lemon

2 cups heavy cream

1/3 cup sugar

2 tablespoons crème de cassis

Candied ginger, chopped, for garnish

Preheat oven to 350 degrees F.

Preparation — Dough:

■ Place the flour, sugar and salt in a food processor and mix for a few seconds. Add the butter and mix for 30 seconds for a crumbly texture; drizzle the heavy cream and pulse briefly. Transfer to a lightly floured cold surface and work quickly with your hands to form a disc. Do not overwork the dough. Wrap in plastic and refrigerate for 30 minutes.

■ Butter and flour 6 personal tartlet pans. When dough is chilled transfer to a lightly floured surface. Flour the rolling pin and roll the dough to 1/8-inch thickness. Cut out 6 dough circles wide enough in diameter to coat the tartlet pans' walls. Chill for 10 minutes. Place parchment paper into each of the tartlets and spread the beans to fill the tartlets. Bake for 15 minutes. Carefully remove the parchment with the beans and bake for 10 minutes until lightly golden. Remove from the oven and let cool.

Preparation — Filling:

■ Heat the milk, ginger and sugar in a saucepot until sugar dissolves. Do not boil. Mix the yolks and the cornstarch in a mixing bowl; pour 1/3 of the milk mixture over the yolk and cornstarch mixture and whisk well. Transfer the yolk mixture back to the pot and reduce to a medium low heat. Stir constantly scorching

the pot's bottom until mixture starts to b[o] and thickens (like a pudding). Add the lemo[n] juice and zest and bring to a boil, stirrin[g] constantly until it thickens again (about 3- minutes). Remove from the heat, pour into th[e] tartlet pans and place in the oven for 5- minutes. Remove from the oven and let cool

■ Before serving, whip the heavy cream an[d] sugar to a soft peak stage. Add the crème d[e] cassis and whip for 10 seconds.

■ Place the tartlet on a small serving plat[e] dust with confectionery sugar and drop [a] dollop of the whipped cream on top. Sprinkl[e] with the candied ginger and serve.

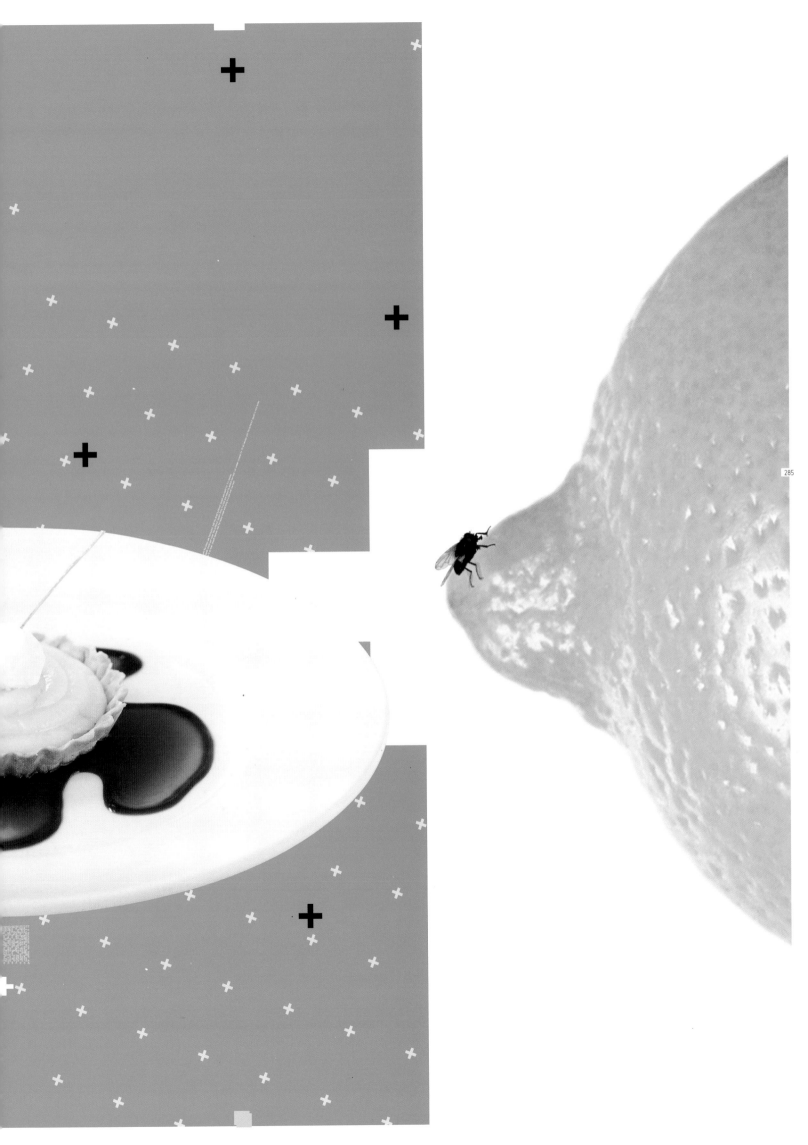

PEANUT BUTTER CRÈME BRULE WITH CHOCOLATE COOKIES

Serves 6

1 quart heavy cream
8 egg yolks
1/2 cup sugar
2-3 tablespoons smooth peanut
butter
Light brown sugar

For the Cookies:

3/4 cup high quality cocoa powder
2 cups flour
1 teaspoon baking powder
1/2 teaspoon salt
8 ounces butter
2 cups sugar
2 eggs
1 teaspoon vanilla extract
Sugar

Preheat oven to 325 degrees F.

■ Heat the milk and sugar in a saucepot until sugar dissolves (milk should not boil). Beat the yolks in a medium mixing bowl, pour 1/3 of the milk over the yolks and mix well. Return the yolk mixture to the pot and stir over low heat for 1 minute. Turn off the heat, add the peanut butter and whisk well. Pour the mixture into 6 brule dishes until 2/3 full. Place the dishes in a deep baking pan and fill the pan with water to cover 2/3 of the dishes' walls. Place in the oven and bake for 40 minutes until set in the middle (when inserting a knife it should come out almost dry). Let cool and refrigerate.

Preheat oven to 350 degrees F.

■ Mix the flour, cocoa powder, baking powder and salt in a mixing bowl. Cream the butter and the sugar in a mixer bowl, using a pedal attachment. Add the eggs and the vanilla extract and mix for 1 minute using a slow speed. Slowly add the dry ingredients to the mixer bowl and combine well. Refrigerate for 30 minutes.

■ Using a small ice cream scoop or your hands roll the dough into small balls. Dip half of it in sugar and place on a baking sheet lined with parchment paper. Bake for 8-10 minutes, let cool.

■ Sprinkle a thin layer of the brown sugar on the Crème Brule and using a small torch, burn the sugar until golden brown (in the absence of a Brule torch, heat a broiler, placing an oven rack as close to the heat as possible and place the Brule dishes under it for 20 seconds). Serve with 2 cookies.

GRILLED BANANAS AND MASCARPONE CREAM NAPOLEON WITH PINEAPPLE SAUCE

Serves 4

For the Twills:

1 pound brown sugar
13 ounces butter
1 pound dark corn syrup
2 1/2 cups all purpose flour
13 ounces almonds, finely chopped

For the Mascarpone Cream:

1 pound Mascarpone cheese

1/3 cup rum
1/3 cup sugar
4 firm bananas
1/3 cup brown sugar
2 ounces melted butter
2 cups unsweetened crushed pineapple
1 tablespoon sugar
1 tablespoon lime juice
1/4 cup pina colada (or pina colada mix

Preheat oven to 350 degrees F.

- Bring the sugar, corn syrup and butter to a boil in a large saucepot. Let boil over medium low heat for 3 minutes. Remove from the heat.

- Mix the flour and the almonds with the syrup, then transfer to a bowl and let cool completely.

- Line a baking sheet with parchment paper or a silk pad. With wet hands make small balls out of the batter and flatten them on the baking pan leaving enough space between each one. Bake for 15 minutes. Transfer from the pan, while still warm, to a flat surface.

- Mix the sugar, mascarpone cheese and rum together with a whisk.

- Slice the bananas on the bias (1/8-inch thick). Brush with the butter and sprinkle with sugar. Heat a grilling pan and when very hot, grill the bananas for 1 minute on each side.

- Heat the crushed pineapple and sugar in a saucepan and add the lime juice. Remove from the heat and mix in the pina colada.

- Place one twill cookie on a plate, along with 2 tablespoons of the mascarpone cream. Spread 3-4 grilled banana slices and top with another cookie. Gently repeat with another layer. A cookie should be placed on top.

- Drizzle around with sauce and garnish with edible flowers.

CREPE WITH VANILLA PASTRY CREAM AND CITRUS SAUCE

Serves 4-6

For the sauce:

For the Crepe:
2 ounces butter
3 ounces flour
2 eggs
1 ounce sugar
Pinch of salt
1 1/2 cups milk
1 tablespoon orange zest

Butter for frying

For the Pastry Cream:
2 cups milk
4 ounces sugar
3 egg yolks
1 vanilla bean
1 1/2 ounces cornstarch

For the Sauce:
1 cup fresh squeezed tangerine juice
1/2 cup fresh squeezed orange juice
2 tablespoons lemon juice
3 tablespoons sugar
1 tablespoon Grand Mariner
2 ounces butter, diced small
Tangerine segments for garnish

Preparation – Pastry Cream:

■ Make a slit in the vanilla bean with a small knife, lengthwise, and scrape some of the vanilla seeds using the dull side of the knife. Place the seeds and bean in a saucepot with the milk and sugar and heat until sugar dissolves (milk should not boil). Beat the yolks in a medium mixing bowl and mix in the cornstarch. Pour 1/3 of the milk over the yolks and mix well; return the yolk mixture to the pot and whisk constantly over medium low heat for 4 minutes until it starts to boil and thickens. Transfer to another dish; cover the exposed cream surface with plastic wrap and let cool.

Preparation – Crepes:

■ Melt the butter in a saucepan until lightly golden. Transfer to a mixing bowl and add the eggs, sugar flour, and salt. While whisking, add the flour and the orange zest (if lumpy, transfer the batter through a sieve). Heat a small nonstick pan and butter it lightly. Ladle some of the crepe batter to the pan swirling the pan to coat evenly. Fry the crepe 1 minute on each side, remove to a plate and repeat with the rest of the batter. The crepes should be as thin as possible.

Preparation – Sauce:

■ Heat a small saucepan for 1 minute over high flame. Pour the citrus juices to the pan and let simmer. Add the sugar and stir; pour the liquor and remove from the heat.

■ Spread 3 tablespoons of the pastry cream in the middle of a crepe, fold in half once, then fold again. Make 2 crepes per serving. Drizzle the sauce on top and around while hot and garnish with the tangerine segments. Serve immediately.

FRUIT TERRINE WITH VANILLA ICE CREAM AND ROASTED PISTACHIOS

Serves 4-6

11/2 pounds firm fruits such as peaches, apricots, pears and plums

3 cups water

1 cup sugar

3 tablespoons lemon juice

1 package unflavored, powdered gelatin (about 2 1/2 teaspoons)

1 pint good vanilla ice cream

2 cups shelled pistachios

2 tablespoons butter, melted

1/2 cup sugar

293

■ Wash the fruits, halve and discard the seeds or pit. Bring the sugar, water and lemon juice to a boil, add the fruits and cook for about 7 minutes. Strain and set 2/3 of the liquids aside.

■ Line a terrine mold with plastic wrap and leave 3 inches of the saran wrap hanging to cover the top. Arrange the fruits, leaving no space, in the terrine dish. The fruits should go a little over the edge of the mold.

■ Mix the gelatin with the liquids and set aside. Transfer to a small saucepan and heat, stirring well, until all gelatins dissolve. Carefully pour the liquid over the fruits, wrap with the saran wrap and place a "weight" on top of the terrine. Refrigerate overnight. Before serving, freeze the terrine for 30 minutes.

Preheat oven to 350 degrees F.

■ Mix the pistachios with the melted butter and sugar. Place on an oiled baking sheet and roast in the oven for about 5-7 minutes until pistachios are caramelized and golden. Remove from the oven. When cooled remove from the pan to a cutting board and break lightly using a rolling pin.

■ Unwrap the terrine and unmold it on to a cutting board. Slice two 1/2-inch slices per serving, using a sharp knife, and place in the middle of a serving plate. Add one scoop of ice cream next to the terrine and sprinkle with the pistachios. Serve immediately.

ESPRESSO PARFAIT WITH MERINGUE CHUNKS
Serves 6

1 1/3 quart whole milk

10 ounces sugar

12 egg yolks

Double portion espresso, very strong or 3 tablespoons instant espresso mixed in 1/3 cup hot water

2 1/2 cups heavy cream

1/2 teaspoon vanilla extract

1/2 teaspoon cinnamon

Preparation – Parfait:

Preheat oven to 350 degrees F.

■ Heat the milk in a saucepot. Whip the yolks and the sugar in a mixing bowl until pale and fluffy. Pour 1/3 of the hot milk over the yolks and whisk, then return the mixture to the pot and cook over low heat, stirring constantly with a wooden spoon, until the mixture is thick enough to coat the back of the spoon. Remove from the

For the Meringue:

5 egg whites

7 ounces sugar

3 ounces finely ground blanched almonds

1 ounce flour

1/2 teaspoon vanilla extract

Coffee liqueur

heat and set aside one cup of the mixture with a ladle. Add the coffee to the remaining mixture in the pot and mix well. Transfer the coffee custard into a mixing bowl and chill over ice.

■ Add the cinnamon and vanilla extract to the 1 cup of plain custard and chill over ice. Store in the refrigerator until serving time. Use as sauce.

■ When the custard is cold, whip the heavy cream to soft peaks and fold into the coffee custard. Pour the custard into personal soufflé dishes, wrap with saran wrap and freeze for 4 hours or overnight.

Preparation – Meringue:

■ Mix the ground almonds and the flour. Whip the egg whites with a third of the sugar until white and foamy; add the rest of the sugar and vanilla extract and continue to whip to almost stiff peaks. Fold the flour mixture into the egg whites. Line a baking sheet with parchment paper and use two spoons to spoon the mixture, with adequate spacing, onto the baking sheet (or use a piping bag) to create "cookies" 1 inch in diameter and about 1/2 inch high. Bake for about 30-40 minutes until dry and lightly golden. Remove from the oven and let cool. When cold, break lightly into big chunks.

■ Run warm water around the walls of the parfait dishes, free the sides with a knife and unmold, upside down, onto a serving plate. Drizzle some of the sauce and coffee liqueur around and top with the meringue chunks. Serve immediately.

ART REFERENCES

PASTA

VEGETARIAN

FISH

POULTRY

- CRISPY DUCK BREAST WITH MANGO RELISH AND YUCCA FRIES:
  "Antibiotic." 197

- PAN-SEARED CHICKEN BREAST WITH GRILLED TOMATILLOS SAUCE AND CORN BREAD:
  "Multimedia". 199

- CHICKEN AND EGGPLANT ROULADES OVER VEGETABLE "SPAGHETTI" IN WARM TOMATO VINAIGRETTE:
  "The Terminator." 201

- CORNMEAL CRUSTED CHICKEN SCALOPPINE OVER LEGUME HASH IN ROASTED RED PEPPER SAUCE:
  Tribute to Fashion. 203

- GRILLED CHICKEN SKEWERS OVER GRILLED ZUCCHINI IN CURRY VINAIGRETTE AND CRISPY NOODLES:
  "Cockfight." 204

- RED CHICKEN THIGHS IN ONION STEW WITH ZUCCHINI CAKES:
  "Curiosity." 207

- ROASTED GARLIC STUFFED CHICKEN BREAST OVER FENNEL CONFIT IN SAFFRON COCONUT MILK SAUCE AND BABY LEAF SALAD:
  "Before and After." 209-210

- SAUTÉED CHICKEN LIVERS NAPOLEON WITH PEARS IN SAFFRON HONEY SAUCE AND PUFF PASTRY:
  Visual Comparison. 212-213

- STIR-FRIED CHICKEN IN PEANUT SAUCE OVER RICE NOODLES AND SAUTÉED SNOW PEAS:
  Tribute to Albert Hitchcock. 215

- BRAISED DUCK LEGS OVER LENTIL RAGOUT AND ROASTED BABY BOK CHOY:
  "Evolution." 216-217

- PAN-SEARED DUCK BREAST WITH BERRY SAUCE, CORN CUSTARD AND FRISEE SALAD:
  "Let's Play." 219

- GRILLED DUCK BREAST OVER CRISPY DICED POTATOES WITH MUSHROOM STEW:
  "Goosedown." 221

- BRAISED TURKEY BREAST WITH TAPANADE STUFFING OVER VEGETABLE RATATOUILLE:
  Tribute to Hieronymus Bosch's "Hell." 222

- BUTTERNUT SQUASH BOATS WITH TURKEY STUFFING, SAUTÉED SWISS CHARD "LASAGNA" IN CHICKEN REDUCTION SAUCE
  "Pac Man." 225

- OVEN-ROASTED CORNISH HENS WITH DATES AND GARLIC STUFFING OVER WILD RICE IN WHITE WINE SAUCE:
  Tribute to Blue Man Group. 227

- GRILLED QUAIL WITH BALSAMIC AND HONEY OVER SPINACH RISOTTO AND BRAISED LEEKS:
  "The Revenge." Michelangelo's David. 229

MEAT

- ON THE COVER:
  "Hunting Season." 231

- SHELL STEAK WITH COLD RICE SALAD AND CHIMICHURRI SAUCE:
  Influenced by Kasimir Malevich's "Black Square" 1913. 233

- ORANGE AND COGNAC BEEF STEW OVER EGG NOODLES:
  "El Matador." 235

- HERBS AND GARLIC ROASTED LOIN OF LAMB WITH ROASTED FINGERLING POTATOES:
  "Metamorphosis." 236-237

- BRAISED LAMB CHOPS IN LEMON SAUCE WITH CORN AND GRAIN CAKES:
  "The Needle." 238-239

- HERB CRUSTED RACK OF LAMB WITH ROASTED PUMPKIN RAVIOLI IN LIGHT VINAIGRETTE:
  "Metal Fringes." 240

- LAMB SHOULDER WITH DRIED FRUIT STUFFING AND SAUTÉED HARICOT VERT
  "Dolly." 242-243

299

- VENISON FILLETS IN POMEGRANATE SAUCE OVER ROASTED PARSNIP AND APPLE PUREE AND WATERCRESS SALAD:
  A tribute to Marcel DuChamps. 246

- PAN SEARED RIB EYE STEAK WITH PORT & BALSAMIC REDUCTION SAUCE OVER BEET AND POTATO LATKES:
  "The General." 249

- HORSERADISH MUSTARD CRUSTED ROAST BEEF WITH WARM POTATO SALAD AND GRILLED TOMATOES:
  Tribute to Francis Bacon. 251

- LAMB KABOBS WITH GREEN TAHINI SAUCE, TOMATO SALAD AND PITA BREAD POINTS:
  "Artificial World." 253

- VEAL SCALOPPINE IN CURRY SAUCE WITH STEAMED WHITE RICE:
  "New Birth." 255

- ROUND STEAK ROLLUPS WITH VERMOUTH SAUCE, SAUTÉED LEEKS AND BUTTON MUSHROOM:
  Tribute to Georgia O'Keefe. 257

- STIR-FRIED BEEF WITH SUN-DRIED TOMATOES OVER ORZO PRIMAVERA:
  ."French Horn." 258-259

- PECAN-CRUSTED VEAL MEDALLIONS OVER BARLEY RISOTTO WITH ONION JAM AND BASIL OIL:
  "Genetics." 261

DESSERTS

300

ACKNOWLEDGEMENT

Firstly I would like to express deep appreciation to my loving wife Mollie for standing behind me throughout the whole making of this book. Deep appreciation also to Emmanuel Paletz's wife Gal Gafni. A huge thank you to Joey Doueck of WILLOUGHBY'S NYC for putting me on my feet to pursue my career I owe it all to you. Thanks to Oren Moshe, Yana Kuzin-Ilan, Yossi Melamed, Steve Rozen, Howard Perl, Marilyn Jefferson, Ellen Linde, Michael Linde, Lisa Marie Meller, The Orchard, Yoseph Friedman, Nir Dubnikov, Jack & Annet Benishai, Yael & Assaf Benishai, Sarit & benny Kimchy, Shane Vardi, Shoshana Kirchenboum, Marketability, Book Tools, Refael Ashkenazi, Motty Benishai, Avi Glatt, Petal Pride, Yakov Bertwain, Ronit & Rami Soosi, Zohar Vilboosh, Zila Paletz, Ruby Gelman, Sami Eyal, Kaufman & Zilberberg, Abrahham Holzberg and last but not least my precious son David Jonathan.

INDEX

303